Praise for *A Child Welfare Worker's Guide to Special Education*

"This manuscript provides a clear, practical, and compassionate road map for child welfare workers navigating special education. With vivid vignettes and actionable guidance, it bridges the gap between policy and practice, equipping readers to advocate effectively for some of our most vulnerable children."

— David Bateman, PhD, Special Education Consultant and Professor Emeritus at Shippensburg University of Pennsylvania, USA

"This guide is an empowering tool for CASAs stepping into the world of special education. It breaks down complex laws and processes into clear, practical language while weaving in vignettes that bring advocacy to life. Every CASA can benefit from the knowledge shared within these pages. We know every child is teachable, and with the right advocacy, every child can learn and thrive."

— Darcy Hubbard, Executive Director of Fairfax Court Appointed Special Advocates, USA

"This text accomplishes something that many do not — it takes a sprawling academic field and reduces it to key themes, definitions, questions, and carefully sampled content and remains coherent and useful. For the student not needing to be an expert in the area, but needing literacy to be effective in their work, this text will be extremely meaningful and useful."

— John Trammel, PhD, Professor and Chair of the Department of Sociology, Criminal Justice and Human Services at Mount St. Mary's University, USA

A Child Welfare Worker's Guide to Special Education

A Child Welfare Worker's Guide to Special Education

Kevin Monnin and
Andrew M. Markelz

BLOOMSBURY ACADEMIC
NEW YORK • LONDON • OXFORD • NEW DELHI • SYDNEY

BLOOMSBURY ACADEMIC

Bloomsbury Publishing Inc, 1359 Broadway, New York, NY 10018, USA
Bloomsbury Publishing Plc, 50 Bedford Square, London, WC1B 3DP, UK
Bloomsbury Publishing Ireland, 29 Earlsfort Terrace, Dublin 2, D02 AY28, Ireland

First published in the United States of America 2026

Cover design by Enterline Design Services
Cover image © iStock.com/Zodchiy, © iStock.com/monkeybusinessimages

A catalog record for this book is available from the Library of Congress.

ISBN: PB: 979-8-2162-0198-4
HB: 979-8-2162-0199-1
ePDF: 979-8-2162-0200-4
eBook: 979-8-2162-0201-1

Typeset by Deanta Global Publishing Services, Chennai, India
Printed and bound in the United States of America

For product safety related questions contact productsafety@bloomsbury.com.

Contents

Figures

Tables

We Have to Do Something

I'm not supposed to see how they line up again and again.
Each card swipe pulls a crowd like roulette at a Vegas casino.
You can't say they aren't engaged—one hand wrapped around
the greasy controller, red button beckoning like the cherry

perched on top of a chocolate sundae, another hand
placed high up on the cabinet for balance, a soft cloud of breath
forming on the glass where a face is pressed close, as if
the distance of a nose will make all the difference.

No matter the skill of each operator, the claw barely obeys commands—
swings around like a noodle dangling on the end of a chopstick.
Each prize plushy looks out with a blank stare, pleading
for a home, so desperate any stranger will do. Everyone circles the case,

shouting advice–closer, farther, too little, too much, aim for the head,
aim for the eye, catch the loop, snag the tail. As the counter falls,
urgent action is required. Cheers build for the crane driver as the claw
hovers over different colors, different fur, the same wanting eyes.

With a sudden press, the cable unfurls—inhales are held. This
is the oldest form of prayer. Will someone pluck a life today
and raise them up? Will we carry them forward? We are involved now
—too close to it, too invested—and by god, I am filled with hope.

I make a simple wish that crane will change a life
—that the claw will hang on.

—a poem by Trapper Markelz

1

An Introduction to Special Education for Child Welfare Workers

Every day, too many US children become victims of child abuse or neglect at the hands of a caregiver. According to the Department of Health and Human Services (2023), in 2022, there were 558,899 child victims of abuse or neglect, of whom 107,747 were removed from their homes and placed into foster care. Of the 368,530 US children in foster care on September 30, 2022 (the most recent national reporting available), the average age of a child in foster care was 8.2, the average time in care was 22.5 months, and a plurality, 44 percent, lived in a non-relative foster home, with 34 percent residing in a foster home in the care of family members or fictive kin (U.S. Department of Health and Human Services, 2023). In the same year, the most common cause for children entering the foster care system was parental neglect, resulting in 62 percent of foster care placements. Parental drug abuse (33 percent), a caretaker's "inability to cope" (13 percent), and physical abuse (13 percent) were the next common causes of separation from the child's home and placement into foster care (U.S. Department of Health and Human Services, 2022). Aside from the considerable trauma of the act of abuse or neglect, the resulting disruption to the child's life, including new caretakers and schools, can all contribute to some of the worst academic and functional outcomes of any demographic group of children (ABA Center on Children and the Law, 2022).

Though the involvement of local child welfare agencies can be a traumatic experience for many children, children in foster care or otherwise involved in the child welfare system, such as those who have some degree of departmental supervision, are often supported by a large group of professionals tasked with making decisions in the child's best interest. In this book, social workers, foster parents, lawyers, and Court Appointed Special Advocates (CASAs) are all considered *Child Welfare Workers* as they work to ensure the child's emotional, social, and academic needs are met. In fact, in 2022, 51,193 child victims had some form of court-appointed representative tasked with making or informing the best interest of the child (U.S. Department of Health and Human Services, 2023). This responsibility often includes making decisions related to their education. As children and youth in foster care are 2.5 to 3.5 times more likely to receive special education services (Jones et al., 2012), these decisions can often involve navigating special education policies and procedures.

Given the stressful nature of their professions and the competing priorities they face, often through no fault of their own, child welfare workers may lack a detailed understanding of the policies and procedures required to obtain effective special education services. This book seeks to remedy that by providing professionals like you with the necessary information to successfully navigate the special education system, improve evidence-based decision-making, bolster advocacy efforts, and enhance child outcomes. Professionals or service providers who may find this book particularly useful include social workers, CASAs, attorneys such as Guardians Ad Litems (GALs), foster parents, and other stakeholders such as case managers, educational advocates, and school counselors. As will be explained in future chapters, collaboration among these and other stakeholders is critical to meet the unique needs of children and youth in foster care.

What Are the Educational Needs of Children in Care?

Researchers have consistently demonstrated that compared to their peers, children in foster care have lower academic achievement, higher rates of school absence, and are subject to greater instances of disciplinary action (ABA Center on Children and the Law, 2022). Furthermore, a lower percentage of foster youth graduate from high school compared to non-foster youth (64 percent vs. 87.3 percent), and even fewer foster care alums attain a bachelor's degree, at 2 percent compared to the 10.8 percent national average (National Center for Education Statistics, 2020). These children and youth, many of whom have experienced abuse and neglect, often grapple with the lasting impacts of trauma and adverse childhood experiences (ACEs), further hindering their educational success. Beyond these, frequent school transfers, difficulty making social connections, a lack of reliable transportation, and financial challenges can all serve as barriers to academic achievement. Addressing these barriers requires a multifaceted approach that goes beyond any one individual intervention. Collaborative efforts between child welfare agencies, schools, and other community partners can serve to strengthen the chances for foster children to thrive in care and beyond and lessen the profoundly negative implications of academic failure.

The American Bar Association's Center on Children and the Law (2022) provides ten research-based practices to support positive long-term outcomes for children and youth in foster care. These include (a) engaging youth in their education, (b) ensuring youth have access to supportive adult advocates, (c) ensuring a strong developmental foundation for young children in care, (d) ensuring stable and timely enrollment in school, (e) promoting regular school attendance, (f) recognizing and addressing childhood trauma, (g) meeting children's special education needs, (h) supporting educational placements for students in residential care, (i) supporting successful graduation from high school, and (j) supporting transitions and the successful completion of post-secondary opportunities. In this book, we will reference or provide insights into all these practices; however, our central objective is to explore in detail how child welfare workers can meet the special education needs of children in foster care or otherwise involved in the child welfare system. We chose this as our primary focus because special education is a field of education guided by legal requirements, including evaluation procedures, formal meetings, timelines, and procedural safeguards. Navigating these legal aspects can be confusing for those not intimately familiar with them. Additionally, children with disabilities are disproportionately represented in the foster care system, and many of these children currently receive or may receive considerable benefits from receiving special education services.

What Are the Educational Needs of Children in Care with Disabilities?

Though sources vary and outdated data limit our ability to determine the precise statistics accurately, it is estimated that between 30 and 50 percent of all US children in foster care have disabilities (ABA Center on Children and the Law, 2022). In contrast, approximately 15 percent of all US children ages 3–21 are identified as having a disability recognized under the Individuals with Disabilities Education Act (National Center for Education Statistics, 2024). The reasons for the overrepresentation of children with disabilities in foster care are not fully known and cannot be definitively linked to one cause; however, prenatal factors such as maternal substance abuse, malnutrition, and untreated infectious diseases have been linked to developmental disabilities (Polloway et al., 2022). Additionally, psychosocial factors may impact the development and manifestation of disabilities. These factors include poverty and socioeconomic status, abuse and neglect, social isolation, and lack of cognitive stimulation (Bradley & Norman, 2022; Polloway et al., 2022).

Regardless of their foster care status, children with disabilities, in the aggregate, perform significantly below their nondisabled peers in reading and math at all grade levels tested by the National Assessment of Educational Progress (National Center for Education Statistics, n.d.). Given the challenges faced by both groups, it is reasonable to assume that children living with the intersectional identity of one who is both disabled and in foster care would have additional barriers to achieving positive educational outcomes. Even so, the impact of disability status extends beyond academic outcomes. Platt and Gephart (2022) found that children in foster care with disabilities had a statistically significantly higher risk of placement disruptions. They found that children with disabilities in foster care spent, on average, 915 days in foster care compared to 514 days for children without a disability. Additionally, they found that Black or American Indian children with disabilities were at the highest risk of having disruptions to placement. Disruptions in placement have the potential to increase educational disruption and school transfers, further perpetuating negative academic and functional outcomes. For children with disabilities in the foster care system, special education and its individualized support, collaborative nature, and legally protected procedural safeguards serve to meet the individualized needs of each child. As such, it can be a powerful structure to improve a child's prospects for a healthy and productive life.

What Is Special Education?

Special education is a specialized field of education designed to meet the unique learning needs of students with disabilities. These needs can vary widely, encompassing a broad range of physical abilities, cognitive functions, and emotional and behavioral characteristics. In the United States, the Individuals with Disabilities Education Act (IDEA) mandates that eligible students receive a Free Appropriate Public Education (FAPE) in the Least Restrictive Environment (LRE). These concepts will be defined in detail in subsequent chapters. In practice, LRE means providing individualized instruction and support to help each student reach their full potential while maximizing their inclusion within the general education setting. Key components of special education include comprehensive evaluations, the development of Individualized Education Programs (IEPs), and ongoing progress monitoring to ensure services are effective.

Individualized Education Programs (IEPs) are legally binding documents that outline a student's specific learning goals, the services they will receive, and how their progress will be measured. These plans are collaboratively developed by a team that includes parents or guardians, educators, related service providers (e.g., speech therapists, occupational therapists), and sometimes the students themselves. As you will find in most chapters, collaboration is a central tenet of special education. The process of creating the IEP aims to create a personalized learning experience that considers the student's strengths, challenges, and individual learning needs. The IEP is not, and *should not* be, considered a static document. Instead, it should undergo regular review and revision to reflect the student's changing needs and progress.

The principle of LRE recognizes that some students may require specialized instruction or support in settings outside of the general education classroom. Placements may be along a continuum of services, including resource rooms, self-contained classrooms, or other specialized settings. The determination of the appropriate educational placement is based on the student's individual needs and the level of support required for them to achieve their IEP goals. These needs and supports are all determined by the IEP team at regularly scheduled meetings. The ultimate goal of special education is to equip students with disabilities with the skills and support they need to succeed academically and ultimately participate fully in society. Since its formalization and implementation in the mid-1970s, special education has provided access to quality education for millions of children with disabilities. Even so, dissatisfaction with the special education system as a whole and the services provided to children in particular has been the subject of much criticism, especially from families (Gershwin, 2022).

In navigating the special education landscape, stakeholders have expressed considerable concerns about the system's complexity and the challenges it presents. Overwhelmed by the implicit and explicit rules, as well as the unique culture of special education, families have frequently described their experiences as isolating and confusing (Choiseul-Praslin et al., 2021). Lacking the necessary knowledge and social capital, many parents face frustration, particularly during IEP meetings (Rossetti et al., 2020). Communication barriers further compound these difficulties, particularly for families whose primary language is not English, as they often struggle without access to adequate translation resources. Additionally, families have reported encountering power imbalances with educational professionals, which can lead to feelings of marginalization and disrespect. Despite legal mandates for family involvement, too many caregivers still feel unwelcome or excluded from meaningful participation in their child's education, hindered by inflexible meeting schedules and a deficit-focused approach. In this book, we aim to equip you with a better understanding of how to navigate these barriers, not just for the children you support, but also for their families, including foster families, adoptive families, fictive kin, and parents who will be reunited with their children. The last point is particularly important as education decision-making authority varies by state. Parents often retain education rights unless those rightsare terminated, they decline, and a surrogate is appointed, or a court order names another decision-maker, such as a child welfare worker.

What Will I Learn from This Book?

To navigate the complexity of special education and bolster your advocacy efforts, we will provide an overview of key components of special education, all of which are relevant to your experience as a child welfare worker. More specifically, we will:

1. Define and explain special education laws, key tenets, and procedures in a thorough yet concise way to aid your advocacy on behalf of children and families.
2. Present realistic examples of advocacy dilemmas in special education that you might encounter through vignettes that highlight prevalent challenges and evidence-based solutions.
3. Provide a coherent understanding of the entire special education process from eligibility to post-secondary transition in a manner that allows chapters to be read in isolation.
4. Share resources that help supplement your reading and can aid your understanding of special education law, procedures, evidence-based practices, and advocacy.

This book is divided into two distinct sections: (1) Information on the foundations of special education and (2) Implementation and practical application of foundational information. In other words, in Section 1, we introduce and define the key elements of special education, and in Section 2, we describe how they are implemented and applied in a realistic context. In Chapter 2, we begin by exploring the historical context of special education, tracing its evolution from exclusionary practices to the current legal framework established by the Individuals with Disabilities Education Act (IDEA). This historical overview highlights key advocates and pivotal legislative changes, setting the stage for understanding the complexities of modern special education. In Chapter 3, we delve into the core principles of IDEA, examining its key components and the interconnectedness of these elements—what we refer to as "the gears of special education"—to support students with diverse needs effectively.

The second section of this book focuses on the practical application of the foundational principles. In Chapter 4, we examine the collaborative nature of the IEP process, identifying key participants and detailing best practices for effective communication and conflict resolution. In Chapter

5, we delve deeply into Individualized Education Programs (IEPs) and 504 Plans, outlining eligibility criteria, key components, and strategies for advocating for high-quality IEPs. In Chapter 6, we examine the crucial role of trauma-informed practices in education, considering the impact of adverse childhood experiences (ACEs), and provide practical strategies for educators and caregivers. In Chapter 7, specific challenges are addressed, including those faced by students with high-intensity needs and those in early childhood special education settings (discussed in Chapter 8), which highlight effective advocacy strategies for these groups of students.

The final chapters focus on transition planning and addressing common challenges encountered during the IEP process. In Chapter 9, we offer guidance on effective transition planning, ensuring continuity of services as students move between grades, schools, or into post-secondary settings. Finally, in Chapter 10, we equip you with strategies to navigate common areas of disagreement among IEP teams, offering methods for conflict resolution and proactive communication to reach consensus and best meet the individualized needs of students in your care. Vignettes and real-world examples will help illustrate core concepts and strategies, enabling effective advocacy for children within the child welfare and special education systems. Whether you are just beginning your role as a child welfare worker or are a veteran in the field looking to deepen your understanding of special education, we hope the following chapters help demystify a complex system and provide you with actionable practices to improve the lives of children and families.

References

ABA Center on Children and the Law. (2022). *Foster care & education data at a glance.* https://docs.fostercareandeducation.org/DesktopModules/Bring2mind/DMX/Download.aspx?portalid=0&EntryId=2134&Command=Core_Download

Bradley, M. R., & Norman, M. E. (2022). The history of the IDEA and its implications for the education of students with disabilities. In J. M. Kauffman, D. P. Hallahan, & P. C. Pullen (Eds.), *Handbook of special education* (3rd ed., pp. 178–195). Routledge.

Choiseul-Praslin, B., Deardorff, M. E., & Yeager, K. H. (2021). Mothers' perceptions of satisfaction, trust, and power in the individualized education program process. *Inclusion, 9*(4), 247–262. https://doi.org/10.1352/2326-6988–9.4.247

Gershwin, T. (2022). Building and maintaining trusting and equitable partnerships with families. In A. Turnbull, H. R. Turnbull, G. L. Francis, M. Burke, K. Kyzar, S. J. Haines, T. Gershwin, K. G. Shepherd, N. Holdren, & G. H. S. Singer (Eds.), *Families and professionals: Trusting partnerships in general and special education* (8th ed., pp. 852–867). Pearson.

Jones, L., Bellis, M. A., Wood, S., Hughes, K., McCoy, E., Eckley, L., & Officer, A. (2012). Prevalence and risk of violence against children with disabilities: A systematic review and meta-analysis of observational studies. *The Lancet, 380*(9845), 899–907.

Polloway, E. A., Patton, J. R., Serna, L., & Bailey, J. W. (2022). *Strategies for teaching learners with special needs (12th ed.).* Pearson.

National Center for Education Statistics. (2020). *Foster and non-foster youth graduation rates in 2019.* https://nces.ed.gov/ccd/tables/acgr_re_and_characteristics_2019-20.asp

National Center for Education Statistics. (2024). *Students with disabilities.* U.S. Department of Education. https://nces.ed.gov/programs/coe/indicator/cgg/students-with-disabilities

National Center for Education Statistics. (n.d.). *Achievement gaps dashboard.* The Nation's Report Card. https://www.nationsreportcard.gov/dashboards/achievement_gaps.aspx

Platt, C., & Gephart, S. M. (2022). Placement disruption of children with disabilities in foster care. *Journal of Pediatric Nursing, 66*, 30–35. https://doi.org/10.1016/j.pedn.2022.05.004

Rossetti, Z., Redash, A., Sauer, J. S., Bui, O., Wen, Y., & Regensburger, D. (2020). Access, accountability, and advocacy: Culturally and linguistically diverse families' participation in IEP meetings. *Exceptionality, 28*(2), 1–16. https://doi.org/10.1080/09362835.2018.1480948

U.S. Department of Health and Human Services, Administration for Children and Families. (2022). *Child maltreatment 2022.* https://www.acf.hhs.gov/sites/default/files/documents/cb/cm2022.pdf

U.S. Department of Health and Human Services, Administration for Children and Families. (2023). *AFCARS report: Preliminary FY 2022 estimates as of May 9, 2023* (Report No. 30). https://www.acf.hhs.gov/sites/default/files/documents/cb/afcars-report-30.pdf

2

A Brief History of Special Education

Thankfully, we live in a world where the equitable treatment and inclusion of students with disabilities in public education are protected by law (Markelz & Bateman, 2022). But this was not always the case. Several decades ago, special education did not exist, and people with disabilities were treated horribly out of misconceptions and ignorance. The history of special education is filled with people and organizations who have advocated for the acceptance, inclusion, and legal protections of people with disabilities. Included in these efforts were not only access to public schools but also equitable treatment within them. Although the progress that students with disabilities experience today has not been easily—nor quickly—gained, the benefits of special education services on academic and life outcomes are undeniable. In this chapter, we will answer the following questions about the brief history of special education:

1. Why were children with disabilities excluded from public education?
2. Who are some key historical advocates for special education?
3. How did special education develop over the decades?
4. What is the Individuals with Disabilities Education Act?
5. Where can I find more information about the history of special education?

Why Were Children with Disabilities Excluded from Public Education?

The founding fathers of the United States agreed that an educated electorate was more desirable and beneficial to a federal democratic republic than an uneducated one. Public education, therefore, became the means by which people in the United States gained a basic level of education. By 1918, every state in the union had a compulsory education law—meaning children of a certain age were required by law to attend some form of education (e.g., public, private, or homeschool). Even though children were required to attend school, as you might have guessed, most children with disabilities were often excluded.

Back in those days, society's understanding of disability was much more limited and ignorant than what it is today. A limited number of schools and programs did exist for students who were deaf, blind, or physically impaired based on the noticeable nature of these disabilities. For example, as early as 1832, the New England Asylum for the Blind was founded. The "typical" cognitive abilities of these populations made it easier for lawmakers and courts to suggest that they could benefit from an education. Many of the thirteen disability categories recognized by the government today (to be discussed later in this chapter), such as specific learning disabilities and autism, were undiagnosed. Often, children with these nuanced neurological disabilities were simply categorized as "feeble-minded" and "idiots" and denied access to education (Arnett et al., 2016).

On the one hand, state governments were mandating that children attend school. However, at the same time, schools were excluding children with disabilities based on their unwillingness to welcome this population without the knowledge and strategies to educate them. This tension between state laws and the protection of children with disabilities under those laws pushed the debate into the courts. Various court rulings, however, maintained the discrepancy between compulsory education laws and the exclusion of children with disabilities. As recently as 1958, the Supreme Court of Illinois, in *Department of Public Welfare v. Hass*, ruled that Illinois' compulsory education legislation did not require the state to provide a free public education for the "feeble minded" or "mentally deficient" because their limited intelligence did not allow them to benefit from a good education (Yell, 2019). A detrimental argument was circulating around court rulings that children with disabilities were "uneducable." If a school could deem a child uneducable, then they could legally exclude that child from an education.

Who Are Some Key Historical Advocates for Special Education?

Unsatisfied with the status quo of exclusion and maltreatment, people and organizations began advocating for the legal and educational protections of children with disabilities (Markelz et al., 2023). At the top of the list were parents and family members.

Parents as Advocates

Mason Fitch Cogswell was a medical physician whose daughter (Alice) fell ill with scarlet fever and subsequently became deaf from the ailment. In the early 1800s, schools for deaf students did not exist; however, Dr. Cogswell was determined to figure out how best to educate his daughter. In 1812, Dr. Cogswell contacted the General Association of Congregational Clergymen of Connecticut to survey the state and determine how many other children were deaf (Martin & Rodriguez, 2022). In total, eighty-four children in Connecticut were identified as deaf. Dr. Cogswell and these parents wanted an education for their deaf children, and it was these parents who advocated for the first school for the deaf in the United States.

Dr. Cogswell partnered with a local clergyman, Reverend Thomas Gallaudet, who traveled to Europe to learn about educating children who were deaf, as no one in the United States had experience. The two returned to the United States and cofounded what is now known as the American School for the Deaf.

Shortly after the school opened, it received a $5,000 grant from the Connecticut General Assembly, making it the first publicly funded school for people with disabilities (Martin & Rodriguez, 2022). Over time, the school's curriculum, based on manual communication, developed into

American Sign Language (ASL). In 1864, Gallaudet's son helped establish the Columbia Institution for the Deaf in Washington, D.C., which is now known as Gallaudet University. What started as one parent wanting an education for his child turned into a group of parents wanting the same thing for their children. This advocacy ultimately led to a new method of teaching, a new language (i.e., American Sign Language, or ASL), and a university for postsecondary education.

Educators as Advocates

While parents were advocating for special education outside school walls, many educators were advocating for the rights of students with disabilities within school walls. One notable educator advocate was Elizabeth Farrell. In the early 1900s, Farrell was teaching at a public school in New York City. At that time, singular intelligence (IQ) testing was used to determine a student's abilities. A low IQ score meant a student had low potential. Farrell advocated for a variety of assessments to determine a student's strengths and interests, which would then be used to develop an individualized curriculum. Farrell developed the concept of specially designed instruction (SDI), which is the foundation of how special education instruction operates today. Farrell also believed that students with disabilities could be educated in an "ungraded class" with the expectation that students could be reintroduced into the general education classroom (Kode, 2017).

Farrell's advocacy for teaching students with disabilities in ungraded classrooms gained momentum. In 1906, she was appointed director of her special education program, officially known as the Inspector of Ungraded Class Department. By 1911, there were over 130 special education (i.e., ungraded) classrooms in New York City. Farrell's advocacy did not stop in New York City. In 1922, she founded and served as the first president of the International Council for the Education of Exceptional Children.

Known today as the Council for Exceptional Children (CEC), CEC is the largest international professional organization dedicated to improving the success of children and youth with disabilities and/or gifts and talents. With over 30,000 members today, CEC advocates for appropriate governmental policies, sets professional standards, provides professional development, and helps professionals obtain conditions and resources necessary for effective professional practice (Council for Exceptional Children, 2022).

Parents of children with disabilities, educators, politicians, and many others saw a society that was excluding children with disabilities from the opportunity of an education. They disagreed with the societal norm that many children were *uneducable* and acted to generate change. Their efforts helped develop special education over the decades.

How Did Special Education Develop over the Decades?

Although court cases, such as *Department of Public Welfare v. Hass* (1958), allowed schools to deny children with disabilities a public education, all that began to change with a pivotal Supreme Court case called *Brown v. Board of Education* (1954), hereinafter referred to as *Brown*. The *Brown* decision took place during the 1950s and 1960s civil rights movement. At that time, many people were advocating for equal opportunity and equal rights for minorities, particularly African Americans. Based on the infamous *Plessy v. Ferguson* (1896) Supreme Court decision that established the "separate but equal" precedent, states were segregating races in schools and denying Black students admission to schools attended by white students. The plaintiffs (i.e., Brown) argued segregation was damaging to the educational opportunities of minorities because segregated schools were not, and could not, be equal. Thus, segregated schools violated Black students' constitutional rights under the equal protection clause of the Fourteenth Amendment. The Supreme Court unanimously ruled in favor of the plaintiff, stating that segregation based solely on an individual's unalterable characteristics (i.e., race) was unconstitutional. The *Brown* decision effectively overturned the "separate but equal" doctrine established in *Plessy v. Ferguson*.

The Supreme Court reasoned in *Brown* that education in our society is of utmost importance. Negative consequences and stigmatizing effects of racial segregation harmed segregated students and denied them equal educational opportunity. The court concluded that segregation based on an individual's unalterable characteristics was unconstitutional (Yell,

2019). Advocates for the inclusion of children with disabilities in public schools seized on the *Brown* ruling and highlighted similarities between the unalterable characteristics of race and disability. If segregating students by race was a denial of equal educational opportunity, then was not the exclusion of children with disabilities also a denial of educational opportunity? The movement for including children with disabilities in schools gained momentum after the *Brown* decision. Societal attitudes and systemic structural change, however, do not happen quickly. It was not until 16 years after the *Brown* decision that two landmark federal district court cases applied the concept of equal opportunity to children with disabilities.

PARC v. Pennsylvania (1972) and *Mills v. Board of Education* (1972)

In *Pennsylvania Associations for Retarded Children (PARC) v. Commonwealth of Pennsylvania* (1972) and *Mills v. Board of Education of the District of Colombia* (1972), the plaintiffs in both cases argued states were disregarding their constitutional obligation to provide equal educational opportunities as supported by the equal protection clause of the Fourteenth Amendment of the Constitution. The *PARC* case was about children with intellectual disabilities being excluded from public education (the term *retarded* was used at the time but is now identified as an *intellectual disability*). However, the *Mills* case was about all children with any type of disability. These cases brought critical concepts involving special education to the forefront:

1. Children with disabilities, regardless of severity, are capable of benefiting from educational programs.
2. Education is not solely defined as an academic experience. Functional life skills (e.g., communicating, feeding, and clothing) are equally important and should be taught in schools when appropriate.
3. Since states had passed compulsory education laws that required children to attend school and mandated free public education, states could not deny children with disabilities access to that education.

The *PARC* and *Mills* cases were decided in favor of the plaintiffs, and the exclusion of children with disabilities from public education was deemed unconstitutional. Because the *PARC* and *Mills* cases were litigated in federal district courts, the rulings only had controlling authority over schools in Pennsylvania and the District of Columbia. However, the persuasive authority of these decisions reverberated across the country. Within a couple of years, forty-six additional lawsuits were filed in twenty-eight states concerning the exclusion of children with disabilities (Zettel & Ballard, 1979). The outcomes of those lawsuits were similar, yet the adequacy of educating students with disabilities across the country varied greatly (Markelz & Bateman, 2022). Eventually, Congress realized the federal government needed to pass comprehensive legislation to protect the rights of students with disabilities. In 1975, the Education of All Handicapped Children Act was passed by Congress and signed into law by President Gerald Ford, establishing the framework for special education as we know it today.

What Is the Individuals with Disabilities Education Act?

> Disability is a natural part of the human experience and in no way diminishes an individual's right to participate in or contribute to society. Improving educational results for children with disabilities is an essential element of our national policy of ensuring equality of opportunity, full participation, independent living, and economic self-sufficiency for individuals with disabilities (Education of All Handicapped Children Act of 1975).

We know that prior to 1975, nearly one million children with disabilities were excluded from public education because schools did not have adequate knowledge, training, and resources to meet their needs. Moreover, children with disabilities were often not even diagnosed. When Congress decided to act, pass legislation, and permanently alter the narrative about disability, they wrote that the purpose of IDEA was to

> ensure that all children with disabilities have available to them a free appropriate public education that emphasizes special education and related

> services designed to meet their unique needs and prepare them for further education, employment, and independent living, to ensure that the rights of children with disabilities and parents of such children are protected, to assist states, localities, educational service agencies, and Federal agencies to provide for the education of all children with disabilities. (IDEA, 2004)

Children with disabilities are only protected under IDEA if they meet IDEA's definition of a student with a disability. IDEA uses a categorical approach to define students with disabilities. Figure 2.1 is a list of thirteen disability categories that students can qualify under, as determined on an individual basis by the school's multidisciplinary team. Over the years, terminologies have changed. For example, in 2010, President Obama signed a law requiring the federal government to replace the categorical term "mental retardation" with "intellectual disability."

It is important to note that not all students with disabilities automatically qualify for protections under IDEA. Because IDEA is about providing educational services, only students whose disabilities adversely impact their education are eligible for special education. A student may have a diagnosed hearing impairment, but if it does not negatively affect their educational progress, they will not qualify for special education. They could, however, receive accommodations with a Section 504 Plan, which we will discuss in Chapter 3.

The Structure of IDEA

Based on the comprehensiveness of the law, IDEA is an extensive 162-page legal document. It is divided into four parts: Part A, Part B, Part C, and Part D. Table 2.1 provides a general overview of each part of IDEA.

IDEA Part A. Any law will have a general provisions section. Within Part A, Congress explains the purpose and goals of the law. Relevant facts regarding the education of students with disabilities are also presented in Part A. It is essential to provide definitions of key terms within any statute to ensure agreement among all stakeholders. These definitions are intended to assist stakeholders in a standard implementation; however, more subjective terms, such as the definition of "appropriate," tend to spark litigation, as we will read about in Chapter 3.

IDEA Part B. Special education teachers and administrators should be familiar with Part B of IDEA. This part addresses the education of students

Categories of Disabilities Under IDEA

- Autism
- Deaf-blindness
- Deafness
- Hearing Impairment
- Intellectual disability
- Multiple disabilities
- Orthopedic impairments
- Other health impairments
- Emotional disturbance
- Specific learning disability
- Speech or language impairment
- Traumatic brain injury
- Visual impairment or blindness

Figure 2.1. Categories of disabilities under IDEA.

with disabilities between the ages of 3 and 21. Part B is by far the largest section of IDEA, accounting for nearly 95 percent of all IDEA expenditures (Congressional Research Service, 2019). To receive Part B funding, states submit special education plans meeting IDEA's requirements. Provisions within Part B require states to ensure that all students who qualify for special education are protected under six key principles, which will be discussed in greater detail in the following chapter. These principles are (a) a free and appropriate public education (FAPE), (b) the guarantee of a nondiscriminatory evaluation, (c) education in the student's least restrictive environment (LRE), (d) an individualized education program (IEP), (e) the right for parent participation in their child's education, and (f) procedural safeguards to protect the interests of students and their families.

IDEA Part C. The importance of early intervention for young children with disabilities is well established in research (National Early Childhood Technical Assistance Center, 2011). Part C of IDEA is crafted to support families and their infants (birth through age 2) with disabilities, or at risk

Table 2.1 The Four Parts of IDEA

Section	Title	Description
Part A	General provisions	Outlines IDEA's general provisions, including the purpose of IDEA and the definitions used throughout the law.
Part B	Assistance for education of all children with disabilities	Includes provisions related to formula grants that assist states in providing a free appropriate public education in the least restrictive environment for children with disabilities ages 3 through 21.
Part C	Infants and toddlers with disabilities	Includes provisions related to formula grants that assist states in providing early intervention services for infants and toddlers birth through age two and their families.
Part D	National activities to improve education of children with disabilities	Includes provisions related to discretionary grants to support state personnel development, technical assistance and dissemination, technology, and parent-training and information centers.

for substantial developmental disabilities. It provides grants to states that implement statewide interagency programs of early intervention services. Services may include training for families, counseling, occupational and physical therapy, speech pathology, medical services, or other services, depending on the individual needs of a family and their child.

Unlike Part B of IDEA, where students receive an IEP, eligible children under Part C receive an individualized family service plan (IFSP). The IFSP is developed among appropriate stakeholders, including the child's family members. It is a guiding document that describes the family's concerns, the child's present levels of function and needs, the services the child and family will receive, where these services will take place, and for how long. A key principle of an IFSP is that services are provided in a natural environment—a place where the family and child are comfortable, usually at home. Early childhood special education services and IFSPs will be examined in Chapter 8.

IDEA Part D. With competitive grants, Part D aims at enhancing the education of children with disabilities on a national level. State Educational Agencies (SEAs) are offered competitive grants to help improve their systems, prepare special education personnel, and enhance education for children with disabilities. Universities and nonprofit organizations are also eligible for competitive grants. Universities typically seek Part D funding for the recruitment and development of special education programs, teachers, and faculty. Grants can support nonprofit organizations in developing information centers and educating parents on various issues, including the importance of early intervention and special education. Less than 2 percent of IDEA funding is directed toward projects under Part D (Congressional Research Service, 2019).

The Effects of IDEA

When IDEA was originally passed in 1975, nearly one million children with disabilities gained access to a free, appropriate public education. Today, IDEA serves more than 7.5 million students, which represents approximately 15 percent of all public school students in the United States (National Center for Educational Statistics, 2024). Figure 2.2 shows students ages 3–21 served under IDEA Part B. The five largest reported percentages of students with disabilities are specific learning disability (SLD; 32 percent), speech or language impairments (SLI; 19 percent), other health impairments (OHI; 15 percent), for example, attention deficit/hyperactive disorder (ADHD), and autism (13 percent). Under IDEA Part C (ages 0–2), 441,515 children with disabilities are served, which is approximately 4 percent of the population (Early Childhood Technical Assistance Center, 2024).

Although students with disabilities were mandated access into public schools in 1975, the equitable inclusion of these students took decades to achieve. In the early years of IDEA, students with disabilities were often segregated into classrooms, tucked away in school basements. Rarely did students with disabilities interact with students without disabilities. Even though IDEA required students to be placed in their least restrictive environment (LRE; discussed in Chapter 3), advocates had to push for rights beyond physical access to school buildings. They needed to advocate for inclusive educational opportunities that advanced students with disabilities socially, emotionally, and academically. Today, more than two-thirds of students served under IDEA spend 80 percent or more of their time during the school day in general education classes among their nondisabled peers. Furthermore, the trend for students with disabilities

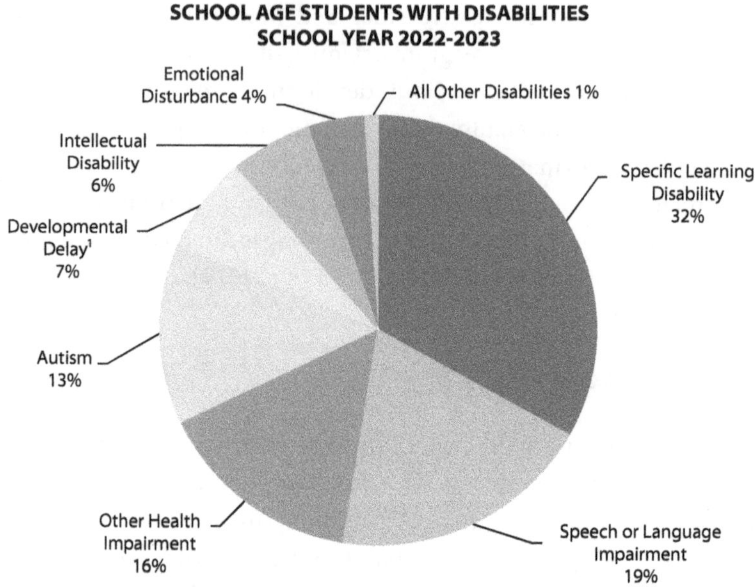

Figure 2.2. School-age students with disabilities. Note: Although federal law does not require that states categorize students according to developmental delay, if this category is required by state law, they are expected to report these students in the developmental delay category. Data obtained from the National Center for Education Statistics (2024).

graduating with a regular high school diploma has been increasing for decades. Fig 2.3).

The positive effects of IDEA for children with disabilities and their families are clear. Societal norms concerning people with disabilities have also improved significantly in terms of awareness, inclusion, and belonging; however, work in these areas remains. Ableism is a term that identifies the discrimination of and social prejudice against people with disabilities based on the belief that typical abilities are superior (Eisenmenger, 2019). Ableism is rooted in the assumption that disabled people require "fixing" and defines people by their disability. Similar to racism and sexism, ableism classifies entire groups of people as "less than" and includes harmful stereotypes, misconceptions, and generalizations of people with disabilities. Thankfully, overt ableist attitudes are less common today. Nevertheless, behaviors and words are often used that imply a disability makes a person less than, or that a disability is bad, negative, and a problem to be fixed. In reality, disabilities are a normal, inevitable part of the human experience.

Contemporary Issues in Special Education

Building on the history we just traced, many of the same pressures and promises still shape what happens in today's classrooms and are closely related to the implementation of IDEA at the state, local, and school levels. These topics have unique implications for children with disabilities in the child welfare system due to their unique intersectional identities and needs. With that context, the following contemporary debates show where those currents surface now and preview issues we examine in later chapters.

Disproportionality in Identification and Discipline. Persistent patterns of overrepresentation and underrepresentation are evident across disability categories and in the use of exclusionary discipline. These patterns intersect with race, language, poverty, and system involvement, producing disparate outcomes for specific student groups. Involvement with the child welfare system may increase the risk of biased referrals when decisions rely on assumptions rather than systematically collected data. To mitigate bias, teams should review local data at regular intervals, implement culturally and linguistically responsive evaluation procedures, and explicitly document how each assessment addresses potential sources of error or bias (National Center for Education Statistics [NCES], 2024; Yell, 2019).

Day-to-Day Discipline, Restraint, and Seclusion. Districts continue to navigate the tension between maintaining safety and implementing preventive, instructional approaches to behavior. Evidence-informed practice prioritizes early intervention through tiered supports, direct teaching of behavioral expectations, staff training in de-escalation, and transparent, routine analysis of discipline data. Where state law permits restraint or seclusion, any use should be limited to situations involving imminent serious harm, followed immediately by debriefing, caregiver notification, and revision of support plans as needed. This approach accords with federal guidance and case law emphasizing the duty to provide FAPE and to avoid disability-based discrimination (Yell, 2019).

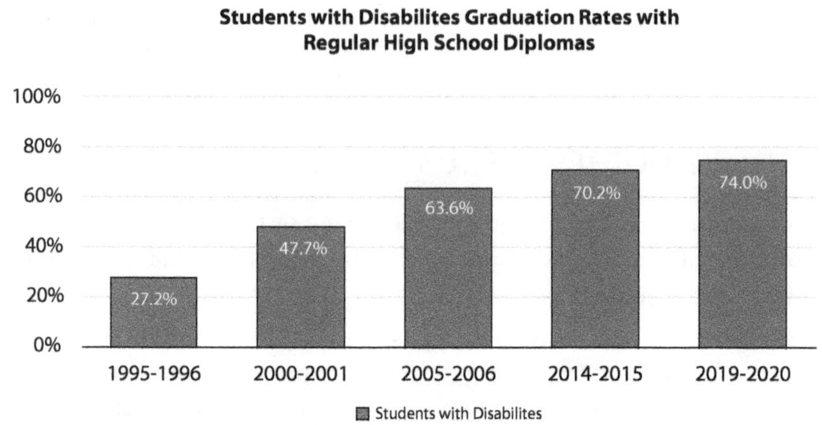

Figure 2.3 Graduation rates of students with disabilities. Data obtained from the National Center for Education Statistics (2024).

Eligibility Decisions and Label Effects. Collaborative teams frequently confront questions about whether a student's needs are most appropriately addressed through eligibility under IDEA categories, such as autism or emotional disturbance, or through a Section 504 Plan. The controlling legal standard is individualized need: services and access barriers must drive the plan rather than the selected disability label. Accordingly, evaluation summaries should make explicit connections between assessment data, functional school impact, and the rationale for the chosen plan type, including why the identified services are necessary to confer benefit or ensure equal access.

Placement Decisions and LRE. Placement is a consequence of services and goals, not a preliminary choice. IEP teams are required to begin with the general education setting and to consider supplementary aids and services before moving to more restrictive options. Any removal from the general setting must be justified with specific evidence tied to the student's needs and the feasibility of implementing the IEP, consistent with IDEA's LRE provisions (Individuals with Disabilities Education Act [IDEA], 2004).

Subsequent chapters examine several of these debates in greater detail. For example, Chapter 6 addresses discipline, trauma-informed supports, and behavior systems. Chapter 5 analyzes plan selection and services under IDEA and Section 504. Finally, Chapter 10 outlines dispute-resolution pathways, enabling readers to move from historical context to practice with concrete tools and examples.

Where Can I Find More Information About the History of Special Education?

- **Book:** *Breakthrough: Federal Special Education Legislation 1965–1981*

  A behind-the-scenes look at the complex array of factors and forces that led to the passage of one of the most important pieces of federal educational legislation in the last fifty years, the Education for All Handicapped Children Act of 1975—now known as the Individuals with Disabilities Education Act (IDEA). Ed Martin's book adds to the historical record. It is a powerful and inspirational reminder to policymakers, advocates, and practitioners in the present why special education is a necessary and noble profession.

- **Video:** *Things People with Disabilities Wish You Knew*

  A short YouTube video of people with disabilities describing common ableist attitudes. https://youtu.be/_b7k6pEnyQ4?si=oXvAwCrxkQhIgRp1

- **Website:** *Council for Exceptional Children*

  The Council for Exceptional Children (CEC) is the largest international professional organization dedicated to improving the success of children and youth with disabilities and/or gifts and talents. https://exceptionalchildren.org/

- **Book:** *Being Heumann: An Unrepentant Memoir of a Disability Rights Activist*

  A story of fighting to belong in a world that was not built for all of us and of one woman's activism—from the streets of Brooklyn and San

Francisco to inside the halls of Washington. *Being Heumann* recounts Judy Heumann's lifelong battle to achieve respect, acceptance, and inclusion in society.

References

Arnett, S., Fitzpatrick, M., & Theoharis, N. R. (2016). *Foundation of special education: Understanding students with exceptionalities*. Kendall Hunt Publishing.

Brown v. Board of Education, 347 U.S. 483 (1954).

Council for Exceptional Children. (2022). About us. *ExceptionalChildren.org*. https://exceptionalchildren.org/about-us

Congressional Research Service. (2019). *The Individuals with Disabilities Education Act (IDEA) funding: A primer*. https://fas.org/sgp/crs/misc/R44624.pdf

Dept. of Public Welfare v. Haas, 154 N.E.2d 265 (Ill. 1958)

Early Childhood Technical Assistance Center. (2024). *Part C national program data*. https://ectacenter.org/partc/partcdata.asp

Eisenmenger, A. (2019, Dec 12). *Ableism 101*. Access Living. https://www.accessliving.org/newsroom/blog/ableism-101/

Individuals with Disabilities Education Act of 2004, Pub. L. No. 108-446, 118 Stat. 2647 (2004).

Kode, K. (2017). *Elizabeth Farrell and the history of special education* (2nd ed.). Council for Exceptional Children.

Markelz, A. M., & Bateman, D. F. (2022). *The essentials of special education law*. Rowman & Littlefield.

Markelz, A. M., Nagro, S. A., Monnin, K., & Bateman, D. F (2023). *The essentials of special education advocacy*. Rowman & Littlefield.

Martin, E., & Rodriguez, J. A. (2022). Historical foundations of special education law: A civil rights movement. In W. Murkowski & J. Rodriguez (Eds.). *Special education law and policy: From foundation to application*. Plural Publishing.

Mills v. Board of Education of the District of Columbia, 358 F. Supp. 866 (D.D.C., 1972).

National Center for Education Statistics. (2024). Students with disabilities. *Condition of Education*. U.S. Department of Education, Institute of Education Sciences. https://nces.ed.gov/programs/coe/indicator/cgg

National Early Childhood Technical Assistance Center. (2011). *The importance of early intervention for infants and toddlers with disabilities and their families.* https://ectacenter.org/~pdfs/pubs/importanceofearlyintervention.pdf

Pennsylvania Association for Retarded Children (PARC) v. Commonwealth of Pennsylvania, 343 F. Supp. 279 (E.D.PA. 1972).

Plessy v. Ferguson, 163 U.S. 537 (1896).

Yell, M. L. (2019). *The law and special education* (5th ed.). Pearson Education.

Zettel, J. J., & Ballard, J. (1979). The Education for All Handicapped Children Act of 1975 (PL 94–142): Its history, origins, and concepts. *Journal of Education, 161*(3), 5–22.

3

The Gears of Special Education

Special education was solidified as a right for children in 1975 with the passage of the Education of All Handicapped Children Act. Today, that piece of legislation has undergone several reauthorizations, court case decisions, and regulatory guidance to strengthen rights, clarify definitions, and improve special education. As discussed in Chapter 2, the Individuals with Disabilities Education Act (IDEA, 2004) has changed the lives of millions of individuals, providing access, opportunity, and equity in education. Six key components of IDEA establish the essence of special education. Often referred to as principles, pillars, or tenets of IDEA, these components are (1) free appropriate public education (FAPE), (2) nondiscriminatory evaluations, (3) least restrictive environment (LRE), (4) parent participation, (5) procedural safeguards, and (6) the individualized education program (IEP).

The primary purpose of IDEA is "to ensure that all children with disabilities have available to them a free appropriate public education (FAPE) that emphasizes special education and related services designed to meet their unique needs and prepare them for further education, employment, and independent living" (IDEA, 20 U.S.C. § 1401 [a][9][A-D]). The law, therefore, centers FAPE as the central component of special education. Although FAPE and the other five components might be considered in isolation, the purpose of this chapter is to demonstrate the interconnectedness of these six components and how they work together to define FAPE for individual students. Figure 3.1 reimagines the six components of IDEA as gears, visually representing the interconnectedness of each gear, with FAPE in the center and the IEP as the largest gear driving all others. In this chapter, we will answer the following questions about the gears of special education.

1. What are the gears of special education?
2. Why do I need to understand the gears of special education?
3. Where can I find more information about the gears of special education?

What Are the Gears of Special Education?

Special education law has procedural and substantive requirements. Procedural requirements refer to the specific steps or processes that must be followed to complete a task. Substantive requirements focus on the content, or substance, of what needs to be done. The procedural and substantive requirements of IDEA essentially define *what* and *how* special education is provided. Each gear of special education has procedural and substantive requirements. A deep dive into each gear of special education is necessary for teachers and administrators, but goes beyond the scope of this book. However, child welfare workers will benefit from knowing the gears of special education because many children under protective services will have a disability and be receiving special education services, or be suspected of having a disability and need special education services. Knowing what each gear of special education is will increase your knowledge and confidence when supporting and advocating for a child under your care.

Free Appropriate Public Education (FAPE)

The spectrum of disability within the human condition is vast. Across the thirteen disability categories qualifiable by IDEA, there are continuums within each disability category from mild conditions requiring minimal support to severe conditions requiring intensive support and complex services. The legislative authors of IDEA understood that special education would be different for each child depending on that child's unique educational needs. Therefore, defining what special education is had to be done on an individual basis. A free, appropriate public education (FAPE)

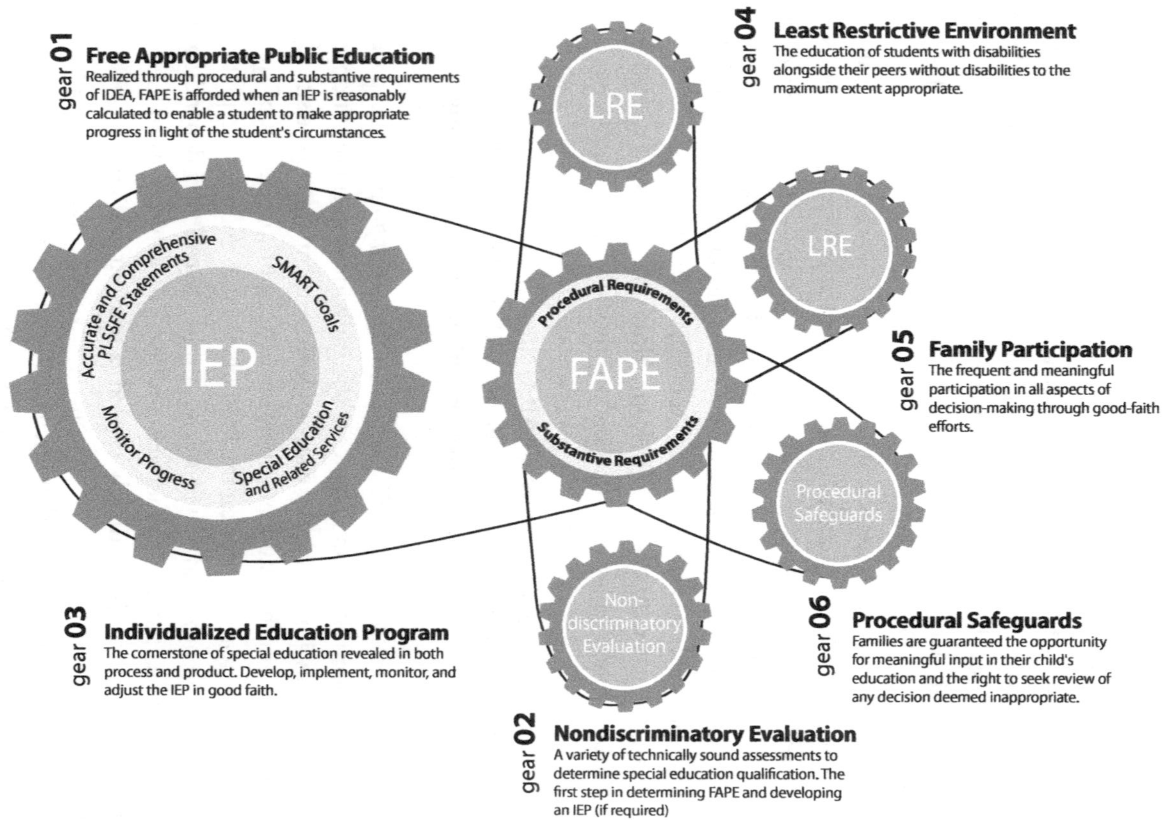

Figure 3.1. The gears of the Individuals with Disabilities Education Act. Gears figure adapted from Markelz et al. (2024).

became the central gear of special education because it allows for that individuality. To best understand the concept of FAPE, we will explore each component, starting with the more objective terms, *free* and *public*. Then we will explore the more subjective term *appropriate*.

Free and Public. All students who qualify for special education under IDEA are entitled to a public preschool, elementary, and secondary education. The school must also provide all special education services at no expense to the family. School fees may be charged to parents of students with disabilities, however, to the same extent that fees are charged to parents of students without disabilities, for example, field trips, art supplies, and technology fees.

A second important aspect of free education is that schools cannot refuse to provide any special education or related services due to the cost of those services. When IEP teams plan a student's special education services, they cannot consider the cost when determining if that service is appropriate. For example, if a student's evaluation concludes that they require physical therapy services, the IEP team must provide these services, regardless of the cost. The only time an IEP team can consider the cost of services is when there are two or more service providers that are appropriate for the student's educational needs. Let's say a student requires applied behavior analysis (ABA) therapy, and there are two local organizations that provide ABA services. Only then can the IEP team consider the cost between the two organizations when making service decisions.

Appropriate. There is no distinct definition of *appropriate* because its meaning depends on circumstances. The individual strengths and needs of one student with a disability can vary greatly compared to the strengths and needs of another student. Therefore, the appropriateness of special education services depends on the individual child, and the interpretation of whether the provided services are appropriate can vary depending on the person (e.g., parent or school personnel). The subjectivity of the term *appropriate* almost immediately caused confusion and conflict between schools and parents. Parents, of course, advocated for higher levels of supports and services so that their children could make meaningful educational progress. Schools resisted due to a lack of training and resources. Since 1975, the US Supreme Court has decided on two cases concerning the definition of FAPE. The first case was *Board of Education of the Hendrick Hudson School District v. Rowley* (1982). The second case was *Endrew F. v. Douglas County School District* (2017). In both cases, the justices attempted to answer the question: What level of educational benefit must school districts provide to children with disabilities to satisfy the free and appropriate public education provision of IDEA? In other words, how does one know whether a student is receiving *appropriate* special education services?

The *Endrew F.* (2017) decision just slightly amended the *Rowley* (1982) decision. The unanimous Supreme Court ruling created a two-part test to determine the obligations of FAPE. The two-part test asks:

1. Has the school district complied with the procedures of the IDEA?
2. Is the IEP reasonably calculated to enable the student to make appropriate progress in light of the student's circumstances?

The first part of the test reinforces *procedural rights* for students with disabilities and their families. If school personnel do not follow the required procedures of IDEA or their state special education laws, a denial of FAPE is likely. For example, schools must complete requested evaluations within a certain timeframe (e.g., 60 days); parents or legal guardians must be invited to join and included on the child's IEP team; and an IEP meeting must take place within 10 school days if a student's educational placement changes. These are just a few examples of specific procedures that school personnel must follow as outlined in IDEA and state special education laws. Procedural requirements tend to be easier to grasp because they are defined and written in law, outlining the procedures to follow.

The second part of the test deals with the *substantive rights* of students with disabilities and their families. This part of the test requires an examination of the substance of a student's IEP to determine whether the IEP is *reasonably calculated* for the student to make *appropriate progress*, considering the *student's circumstances*. The substantive rights of IDEA are where the individuality of special education really emerges. As the other gears are examined, the substantive requirements of FAPE become apparent.

Nondiscriminatory Evaluation

As previously stated, it is challenging to discuss each gear in isolation as they all contribute to the procedural and substantive requirements of FAPE (see Figure 3.1). But starting with nondiscriminatory evaluations is a good place, as this gear illuminates the "student's circumstances." Before an IEP team can "reasonably calculate" the student's IEP or determine if the student is making "appropriate progress," they must have a holistic understanding of the student. What are the student's strengths? What are the student's areas of need? What does the student like and not like to do? What are the student's goals and ambitions? What are the student's family's hopes and dreams for their child? Moreover, to what degree does the student's disability impact their education? All of these questions, and more, begin to construct an understanding of a student's circumstances.

A nondiscriminatory evaluation is a process not biased for or against any individual or group of students and is the first step in determining FAPE (Markelz & Bateman, 2022). For a student to qualify for special education services, they must first have a disability within one or more of the thirteen disability categories outlined in IDEA, and that disability must have a negative impact on the student's education. There are many procedural requirements of a nondiscriminatory evaluation process that extend beyond the scope of this book; however, a few examples of procedural requirements are (1) evaluations are administered by trained personnel, (2) multiple valid and unbiased assessments are used to evaluate all areas related to the suspected disability, (3) assessments are provided in the student's native language, and (4) a response to intervention (RTI) model is used for identifying specific learning disabilities. For a school team to meet the procedural requirements of a nondiscriminatory evaluation, it must follow these and other procedures outlined in IDEA and state special education laws.

The nondiscriminatory evaluation substantively contributes to FAPE by gathering all the information needed to identify the student's circumstances, which directly translates into developing an accurate and comprehensive present level of academic achievement and functional performance (PLAAFP) statement within the IEP. This component of the IEP may go by other names, including the "PLOP: Present Level of Performance." A well-crafted PLAAFP statement summarizes all aspects of a student's present levels of performance in order to identify the student's baseline level of functioning or progress. The PLAAFP statement must contain comprehensive details so that IEP teams can (a) develop appropriately ambitious, measurable, annual goals that promote student growth; (b) determine special education services; and (c) measure student progress (Harmon et al., 2020).

Individualized Education Program

The IEP is represented in Figure 3.1 as the largest gear because it is the means by which a student's FAPE is developed, documented, and delivered (Bateman, 2017). A student's FAPE is realized within their IEP because all aspects of the student's special education are led and monitored throughout the IEP process. While all gears contribute to FAPE, they are also integral to the procedural and substantive requirements of the IEP.

A few examples of procedural requirements of the IEP include adhering to required timelines (e.g., progress monitoring and annual reviews), ensuring attendance at IEP meetings by all necessary team members, and implementing special education and related services as written in the IEP (e.g., if transportation is written as a related service, transportation must be provided).

The substantive requirements of an IEP are provided in Figure 3.1 on the inside of the gear. As mentioned under nondiscriminatory evaluations, accurate and comprehensive PLAAFP statements are the foundation of a substantive IEP. The PLAAFP statement identifies who the student is and what they need regarding special education. An IEP cannot be "reasonably calculated" without an accurate and comprehensive PLAAFP statement. From there, the IEP team can develop specific, measurable, attainable, relevant, and time-bound (SMART) goals (Hedin & DeSpain, 2018). Based on input from IEP team members (including family and case workers), the IEP team sets annual SMART goals that are individualized and tailored to the student's circumstances. Once a complete list of goals has been developed, the team determines the level of special education and related services needed to "make appropriate progress" toward those goals. Decisions are made such as the intensity and setting of specially designed instruction, accommodations on assessments, and related services and supplemental aids.

The IEP team might believe that the IEP is reasonably calculated for the student to make appropriate progress given the student's circumstances. However, the team cannot know for sure without one final critical component of the substantive requirements of an IEP and FAPE: progress monitoring. Data collection on whether the student is making appropriate progress toward their annual goals is the only way to verify whether the IEP is reasonably calculated. If regular data collection shows that the student is making progress toward their annual goals, then that is great!

The IEP team can continue delivering the IEP as planned. If, however, the student is not making adequate progress, then the IEP team must meet and discuss necessary changes to recalculate the IEP. Systematic progress monitoring is an essential substantive requirement that shows a data-based, data-driven IEP is reasonably calculated to enable the student to make appropriate progress (Markelz & Bateman, 2022). The extent of progress, or what is deemed appropriate, can only be determined by the student's individual circumstances.

The substantive requirement of FAPE, as determined by the Supreme Court in *Endrew F.* (2017), created a circular process for defining FAPE. Given the individuality of every student with a disability, an exact definition of what is, or is not, an appropriate education is impossible. What is possible is an individual definition determined by each IEP team based on each student's individual circumstances.

Least Restrictive Environment

Due to the historical segregation of people with disabilities, advocates urged Congress to include measures in the initial passage of IDEA that would require schools to educate students with disabilities alongside their nondisabled peers (Yell & Christle, 2017). An amendment was added to the final piece of legislation and became known as the Least Restrictive Environment (LRE) mandate. The LRE mandate is a fundamental concept protecting the rights of students with disabilities. The IDEA (2004) specifically states:

> To the maximum extent appropriate, children with disabilities, including children in public or private institutions or other care facilities, are educated with children who are not disabled, and that special classes, separate schooling, or other removal of children with disabilities from the regular educational environment occurs only when the nature or severity of the disability is such that education in regular classes with the use of supplementary aids and services cannot be achieved. (34 C.F.R. § 300.114[a][2] [i-ii])

Although the LRE mandate requires schools to place students in the least restrictive settings (i.e., alongside their nondisabled peers), that may not be the most appropriate setting for a student to receive FAPE. The two special education pillars of LRE and FAPE are, therefore, interconnected yet sometimes in conflict (Markelz & Bateman, 2022). Given that special education is about the educational progress of a student, the appropriateness of that education (i.e., FAPE) supersedes the restrictiveness of an environment (i.e., LRE). In other words, schools must strive to educate students with disabilities in less restrictive settings; however, the appropriateness of that setting can only be determined by whether the student can make appropriate progress given their circumstances.

The procedural requirements of determining a student's appropriate placement along the continuum of settings is an important process for IEP teams to follow. After the team has developed annual goals within the IEP, they are required to first consider the general education classroom as a setting for the student to receive special education services. Depending on the student's circumstances and goals, if the general education classroom is deemed inappropriate, the team works down the continuum of restrictive placements to determine the most appropriate placement. The IEP team must balance the LRE mandate and the student's individual FAPE when reasonably calculating their IEP.

To clarify the potential tension between LRE and FAPE, some scholars have suggested that a more useful term than LRE is the least restrictive *appropriate* environment (Yell & Prince, 2022). The least restrictive appropriate environment requires the IEP team to consider the student's progress toward their goals through the use of special education services while being educated in the placement that will confer FAPE. The LRE gear contributes to FAPE procedurally and substantively in important ways. It is also integral to the meaningful and legally defensible development and delivery of IEPs. Predetermination is a common procedural and substantive violation with LRE (Yell et al., 2020) where a student's placement is determined based on convenience, lack of resources, or means other than the student's individual circumstances, goals, and special education needs. To avoid predetermination, IEP teams must intentionally consider the individual circumstances and needs of each student before making a placement. Then, progress monitoring is again critical in measuring whether the IEP is reasonably calculated as the student makes appropriate progress toward their goals.

Family Participation

The fifth gear is family participation, which also contributes procedurally and substantively to the requirements of FAPE. An IEP is a legal document between a school and a family that outlines the special education services to be provided in good faith. Families of students with disabilities, including parents and/or legal guardians, play a vital role as IEP team members in the development, documentation, and monitoring of the child's IEP. Within IDEA (2004), "parent" is broadly defined as (a) a biological or adoptive parent, (b) a foster parent, (c) a guardian authorized to act as the child's parent, d) an individual acting in place of a parent (including grandparent, stepparent, or other relative), or e) a surrogate parent who has been appointed. Table 3.1 outlines the specific roles and permissions of parents and other child welfare with regard to education decision-making. Table 3.1

When considering the substantive requirement of FAPE, who is better to help identify a student's circumstances than someone who knows what is going on at home? Through meaningful participation in the evaluation process and IEP development, parents, foster parents, Court Appointed Special Advocates (CASA), and child welfare workers can all contribute to the substantive quality of the child's IEP. Their input must be considered when developing annual SMART goals and reasonably calculating the IEP to meet those goals. Parent participation, however, does not mean that parents have absolute authority over placement, program, and related services. Parents are not superior members of an IEP team; rather, they are equal partners.

To ensure that parents are active members of the IEP team, there are several procedural requirements under IDEA regarding family participation. The most basic procedural requirement involves notification. School personnel must notify all members of the IEP team in advance when an IEP meeting is approaching. Families must be notified if any changes to the IEP are being considered. School personnel need to have open and frequent communication with families or legal guardians because this allows them to be active members in the IEP process, which in turn enables them to make substantive contributions to IEP development and monitoring.

Procedural Safeguards

The Fifth and Fourteenth Amendments of the US Constitution declare that no state may deprive any person of life, liberty, or property without due process of law. When Congress passed IDEA in 1975, it wanted to

Table 3.1 Roles and Permissions Matrix (K–12 Special Education)

Role	Request Evaluation	Consent to Evaluate	Provide/Receive Records	Attend Meetings	Sign IEP / Consent to Services	File Dispute (State Complaint / Due Process)
Parent / Legal Educational DecisionMmaker	Yes	Yes	Yes	Yes	Yes	Yes
Foster Parent	Often yes	Only if recognized as the "parent" under IDEA or specifically authorized[a]	With consent or if acting as "parent;" otherwise consent/court order	Yes	Only if recognized/ authorized[a]	State complaint: sometimes; Due process: only if the foster parent is the IDEA "parent"/ appointed ED decision-maker[b]
State Caseworker	Yes (refer/share concerns)	No (unless appointed as ED decision-maker/ surrogate)	May receive under FERPA's child welfare exception when the agency has legal responsibility; redisclosure limits apply[d]	Yes (if invited/ role-based)	No	State complaint: agency may file in some states; Due process: typically no (unless acting as the "parent")[b]

(Continued)

Table3.1 (continued)

CASA / GAL	May ask team to consider issues	No	Observations only unless parent consent or specific court authority; CASAs are generally not "school officials" under FERPA[e]	Yes (if permitted by order/ policy)	No	State complaint: sometimes (as an individual/ organization). Due process: No unless appointed as the "parent"[b]
Student	May self-refer (age-dependent)	Age/rights dependent (rights may transfer at age of majority)[c]	Yes, once rights transfer; otherwise via parent	Yes	Age/rights dependent[c]	Where rights have transferred[c]
School Staff / District	Yes	N/A	Yes (FERPA-permitted within the district)	Yes	No (district is not the "parent")	Both (district may file state complaint or due process)[b]

Note. Authority varies by state law, court orders, and district policy. Always verify who holds educational decision-making rights before seeking consent or sharing records. Specific notes. [a]"Parent" under IDEA may include a foster parent when allowed by state law and not prohibited by agency contract; the IDEA definition controls consent authority (34 C.F.R. § 300.30). [b]A parent or a public agency may file due process complaints; state complaints may be filed by any individual or organization (34 C.F.R. §§ 300.507, 300.153). [c]IDEA rights may transfer to the eligible student at the age of majority as provided under state law (34 C.F.R. § 300.520). [d]FERPA, as amended by the Uninterrupted Scholars Act, permits disclosure of education records to child-welfare caseworkers or representatives when the agency has legal responsibility for the student's care and protection; redisclosure limits apply (U.S. Department of Education, 2014). [e] CASAs/GALs generally require parent consent or a specific court order to access education records; absent strict control by the school/district, they are not "school officials" for FERPA purposes (U.S. Department of Education, FERPA FAQ).

guarantee that educational provisions for students with disabilities and their families were protected under due process principles. It was premeditated that disagreements between families and schools would arise over special education services. Therefore, procedures and policies needed to be put in place to remedy such disagreements.

According to the US Supreme Court, procedural safeguards were established in IDEA to "guarantee parents both an opportunity for meaningful input into all decisions affecting their child's education and the right to seek review of any decision they think inappropriate" (*Honig v. Doe*, 1988, p. 598). More recently, the US Supreme Court stated, "an IEP must be drafted in compliance with a detailed set of procedures...." These procedures emphasize collaboration among parents and educators and require careful consideration of the child's individual circumstances" (*Endrew F. v. Douglas County School District*, 2017, p. 2). The IDEA is specific about what schools must do procedurally to ensure that parents or legal guardians have an active voice in the entire special education process, if they want. Those procedural requirements directly contribute to the substantive requirements of reasonably calculating an IEP to enable the student to make appropriate progress in light of the student's circumstances.

Why Do I Need to Understand the Gears of Special Education?

Alarming data suggest the rate of child abuse and neglect is at least three times higher in children with disabilities than in children without disabilities (Jones et al., 2012). Children with disabilities are more frequently referred to child protective services, found to have been abused, and placed in foster care (Kistin et al., 2016). These statistics do not even include the number of children who are in child protective services without a documented disability but are at risk due to correlated evidence between traumatic childhood experiences and developmental delays (Shonkoff et al., 2012). It is almost certain that if you work in the child protective service field, are a foster parent, or a CASA volunteer, you will encounter a child with a disability or suspected of having a disability. The disability(s) may be difficult to identify, such as a mild learning disability. Alternatively, it could be more apparent, like a significant intellectual disability. It is highly likely that a child with a disability under child protective services will be, or should be, receiving special education services.

Special education is defined by the IDEA and decades of case law, which can cause challenges for those unfamiliar with it. As this and other chapters discuss, there are numerous acronyms, technical jargon, and legal complexities that can intimidate and prevent child welfare workers from understanding special education and effectively advocating for the child(ren) on their case. Understanding the gears of special education is the first step in grasping the function of special education. As the US Supreme Court stated, to meet the obligations of IDEA, schools must follow the procedures and offer an IEP that is reasonably calculated to enable the student to make appropriate progress in light of the student's circumstances (*Endrew F v. Douglas County School District*, 2017). Each gear contributes to identifying and documenting the student's circumstances. Each gear contributes to reasonably calculating the IEP based on the student's circumstances. Moreover, each gear contributes to determining whether the student is making appropriate progress, given their circumstances.

As was highlighted throughout this chapter, the IEP is the driving gear behind special education. Understanding the components of the IEP and being an active participant on the IEP team is a crucial role for child welfare workers. In Chapters 4 and 5, we will present how to be knowledgeable and an effective advocate in that role.

Where Can I Find More Information About the Gears of Special Education?

- **Website:** *Understood.org*

  www.Understood.org is a nonprofit organization empowering the seventy million people in the United States with learning and thinking differences. They provide free, expert-vetted resources and support so people who learn and think differently can thrive in school, at work, and throughout life.

- **Video:** *IDEA Basics: Free Appropriate Public Education*

  A short YouTube video featuring two special education attorneys discussing the meaning of "free and appropriate public education" (FAPE). https://www.youtube.com/watch?v=ElusLM-WVtA

- **Book:** *The Essentials of Special Education Law*

  This book distills the legal complexities of special education law into a practical resource for professionals in the field.

- **Website:** *Center for Parent Information & Resources*

  www.parentcenterhub.org is the central hub for valuable information and products specifically designed for the network of Parent Centers that serve families of children with disabilities.

References

Bateman, B. D. (2017). Individualized education programs. In J. M. Kauffman and D. P. Hallahan (Eds.), *Handbook of special education* (2nd ed., pp. 91–124). Taylor & Francis/Routledge.

Board of Education of the Hendrick Hudson School District v. Rowley, 485 U.S. 176 (1982).

Endrew F. v. Douglas County School District, 137 S. Ct.. 988 (2017).

Harmon, S., Street, M., Bateman, D., & Yell, M. L. (2020). *Developing present levels of academic achievement and functional performance statements for IEPs*. Teaching Exceptional Children, 52(5), 320–332. https://doi.org/10.1177/0040059920914260

Hedin, L., & DeSpain, S. (2018). SMART or not? Writing specific, measurable IEP goals. *Teaching Exceptional Children, 51*(2), 100–110.

Honig v. Doe, 484 U.S. 305 (1988).

Individuals with Disabilities Education Act of 2004, 20 U.S.C. § 1400.

Jones, L., Bellis, M. A., Wood, S., Hughes, K., McCoy, E., Eckley, L., . . . & Officer, A. (2012). Prevalence and risk of violence against children with disabilities: A systematic review and meta-analysis of observational studies. *The Lancet, 380*(9845), 899–907.

Kistin, C. J., Tompson, M. C., Cabral, H. J., Sege, R. D., Winter, M. R., & Silverstein, M. (2016). Subsequent maltreatment in children with disabilities after an unsubstantiated report for neglect. *JAMA, 315*(1), 85–87.

Markelz, A. M., & Bateman, D. F. (2022). *The essentials of special education law*. Rowman & Littlefield.

Markelz, A. M., Nagro, S. A., Monnin, K., & Bateman, D. F (2024). *The essentials of special education advocacy*. Rowman & Littlefield.

Shonkoff, J. P., Garner, A. S., Committee on Psychosocial Aspects of Child and Family Health, Committee on Early Childhood, Adoption, and Dependent Care, and Section on Developmental and Behavioral Pediatrics, Siegel, B. S., Dobbins, M. I., Earls, M. F., . . . & Wood, D. L. (2012). The lifelong effects of early childhood adversity and toxic stress. *Pediatrics, 129*(1), e232–e246.

U.S. Department of Education. (2014). *Uninterrupted Scholars Act*. https://www.ed.gov/sites/ed/files/2020/09/Uninterrupted-Scholars-Act.pdf

Yell, M. L., & Christle, C. A. (2017). The foundation of inclusion in federal legislation and litigation. In C. M Curran & A. J. Petersen (Eds.), The *handbook of research on classroom diversity and inclusive education practice* (pp. 27–52). IGI Global.

Yell, M. L., Katsiyannis, A., Ennis, R. P., Losinski, M., & Bateman, D. (2020). Making legally sound placement decisions. *TEACHING Exceptional Children, 52*(5), 291–303.

Yell, M. L., & Prince, A. T. (2022). Why the continuum of alternative placements is essential. In J. M. Kauffman (Ed.), *Revitalizing special education* (pp. 59–78). Emerald Publishing Limited.

4
Collaboration in Special Education

Just as is the case with the field of child welfare, collaboration is not merely a suggestion in special education; it is the bedrock upon which effective Individualized Education Programs (IEPs) are built. The Individuals with Disabilities Education Act (IDEA) emphasizes a shared responsibility among various stakeholders to meet the unique needs of students with disabilities. This chapter examines the collaborative nature of special education, including IEP development and implementation, and highlights the roles of key participants. It also offers practical strategies for effective teamwork. We will use a fictional vignette to illustrate these concepts, focusing on the importance of communication and proactively building relationships with stakeholders. In doing so, we will answer the following questions:

1. Who will you interact with in special education meetings?
2. How is your role in the special education process different from that of a parent?
3. What are some best practices in collaboration?
4. Where can I find more information about collaboration in special education?

Sarah, a recently appointed Court Appointed Special Advocate (CASA), has accepted her first case: a fourth-grade student named Alex. He is struggling academically, particularly in reading and math, and exhibits disruptive behaviors in his classroom. Alex lives with his grandmother, Ms. Jones, who is overwhelmed by his challenges and feels lost navigating the special education system. Alex has been in the care of the Department of Children and Family Services (DFS) since last summer when he was removed from the care of his mother and stepfather for allegations of physical abuse. At the age of five, he was identified as needing special education due to developmental delay. Since then, he has been found eligible under the category of Learning Disabilities.

Ms. Jones has struggled to manage his difficult behavior at home. Still, she is primarily concerned with his academic progress and ensuring he can remain at his current school for years to come. She recognizes that he has had a lot of disruptive transitions and traumatic experiences in his life, and she is adamant that his behavior does not cause his expulsion from his current school. She tells Sarah all of this when the CASA calls her to introduce herself and explain her role. Ms. Jones shares with Sarah that Alex's mother recently relinquished her parental rights and has since moved out of the state. After his removal from his mother's house, Ms. Jones has served as his foster mother, but she intends to adopt him as soon as she "gets her paperwork in order." His grandmother also explains that she received a call from the school, letting her know that his IEP is to be renewed and revised next week. The school team thinks this is a good time to address recent academic and behavioral challenges. Ms. Jones explains that she has never attended an IEP meeting and is unsure of what to expect. She wants to be prepared but is concerned she will be overwhelmed by the procedures. "Who will be there?" she asks. Sarah remains quiet because she has the same questions.

Who Will You Interact with in Special Education Meetings?

In special education meetings, particularly during the development of an Individualized Education Program (IEP), various participants come together to discuss the student's educational needs (see Figure 4.1). Many of these participants are required to be in attendance per the regulations set forth in IDEA. Understanding the roles and contributions of each participant is essential for effective collaboration, as it allows everyone involved to work toward a shared goal of supporting the student's educational journey.

Key Participants in Special Education Meetings

The Student's Parent(s), Guardian(s), or Caregiver(s). IDEA defines a parent as a natural, adoptive, or foster parent of a child (unless a foster parent is prohibited by state law), a guardian (not including the state if the child is a ward of the state), an individual acting in place of a natural or adoptive parent, or an individual assigned to be a surrogate parent (IDEA, 2004). Parents, or the more inclusive term, caregivers, play a pivotal role in the IEP process. Importantly, those with parental rights retain the right to make educational decisions under most circumstances. The nuances of these circumstances will be discussed in subsequent sections. Caregivers often provide critical insights into the child's strengths, needs, and home environment. Their knowledge about the child's experiences, preferences, and aspirations is invaluable for developing a comprehensive IEP. Caregivers' participation ensures that the IEP reflects the child's circumstances, promotes their best interests, and aligns with their personal goals. Importantly, parents can stop the implementation of all or part of the IEP if they find it is not appropriate for their student.

Special Education Teacher. The special education teacher is responsible for delivering specially designed instruction and supports to meet the unique needs of students with disabilities. In addition to their instructional responsibilities, special education teachers commonly serve as case managers. As a case manager, the special education teacher's role is to coordinate and oversee the special education services, including scheduling meetings, documenting progress toward IEP goals, and bridging communication gaps between parents, teachers, and related service providers. Special education teachers bring expertise in teaching strategies, accommodations, and modifications that are necessary to help students succeed. Their understanding of special education best practices and procedures is integral to the IEP process. Moreover, they often serve as the primary contact for parents regarding the implementation of the IEP and any adjustments that may be needed over time.

General Education Teacher(s). A general education teacher contributes to the IEP by providing insights into the student's performance in the general curriculum. As mentioned in previous chapters, the LRE mandate ensures, to the greatest extent possible, that

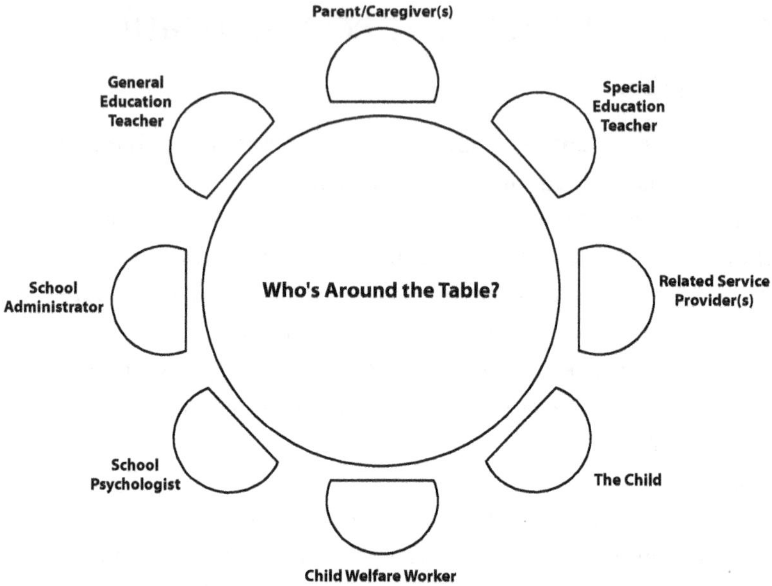

Figure 4.1. IEP meeting participants.

children with disabilities are educated alongside their nondisabled peers. Oftentimes, this is the general education setting. As such, the general education teacher is an important voice in explaining the child's progress in accessing the general education curriculum. By sharing observations about the child's interactions with peers and their engagement in classroom activities, the general education teacher helps create a holistic understanding of the child's educational experience. Their collaboration ensures that the IEP is aligned with the expectations of the general education curriculum. They also provide support within their classroom to help integrate the student effectively alongside their peers.

School Administrator. A principal, special education coordinator, or someone designated by the principal to serve as their representative is required to attend IEP meetings to ensure that the school complies with special education regulations and provides the necessary resources and support for implementing the IEP. Their leadership role is crucial in fostering a collaborative culture within the school and promoting inclusion and support for students with disabilities. Administrators also play a key role in facilitating training and professional development opportunities for staff to enhance their understanding of special education policies.

Potential Participants in Special Education Meetings

Related Service Providers. These specialists, such as speech-language pathologists, occupational therapists, and physical therapists, provide essential services that support students' learning and development. Their contributions are vital in addressing specific needs that may impact the child's educational success. For instance, a speech-language pathologist may work on communication skills, while an occupational therapist may focus on fine motor skills necessary for completing written assignments. Related service providers often only attend IEP meetings for students with whom they are currently working or for students who may be eligible for their services. For these instances, collaborating with these professionals is critical to ensure that services are coordinated effectively and integrated into the student's overall education plan.

School Psychologist. School psychologists play a crucial role in the assessment process, providing insights into behavioral strategies and mental health support. In addition to their role in the initial evaluation of children, school psychologists may conduct assessments to identify the student's strengths and challenges, which can inform the IEP. Additionally, they serve as a valuable resource for other team members, including parents, in explaining the results of assessments and their implications. Particularly for students in care, their expertise in understanding social-emotional development is useful for ensuring that the child's emotional and psychological needs are addressed. Additionally, they can serve as a resource for training general and special education teachers on recognizing and managing behavioral issues in the classroom.

Child Welfare Worker. As a child welfare worker, your role is to advocate for the child's well-being and ensure that their educational needs are recognized and addressed. You serve as a bridge between the child's home life and the school environment, bringing a unique perspective that focuses on the child's overall welfare, safety, and educational success. Many of your children may have transferred between placements or schools several times, making it even more important for you to be able to adequately explain their education history, including past services, progress, and placements as needed. When advocating for a child's needs, ensure that their voice is heard and that their best interests are prioritized during meetings.

The Child. When appropriate, particularly as children age, attending their own IEP meeting can be a beneficial opportunity for them to explain their thoughts on services, accommodations, modifications, and placements. Participation in developing their own IEP allows children to gain a sense of ownership over their education and develop essential communication skills as they articulate their needs and preferences. This involvement fosters confidence, enhances their understanding of goals and services, and prepares them for future transitions, while promoting collaboration among the child, parents, and educators. Although there is no definitive age at which IEP attendance should begin, students are required to start actively contributing to their transition planning by the time they turn 16. Many states encourage IEP attendance and transition planning to start around age 14. We will discuss transition planning in detail in Chapter 9.

Others. A variety of other stakeholders can attend IEPs, including anyone invited to the meeting who has knowledge or special expertise regarding the child. Paid or volunteer advocates, therapists, service providers, and/or lawyers are often examples of invited attendees at IEPs. Regardless of who you interact with at an IEP, it is important to ensure you are maintaining confidentiality and safeguarding sensitive information.

Confidentiality is foundational to effective collaboration between stakeholders and lawful practice. Specific rules on confidentiality likely vary based on your particular role; however, certain key tenets of confidentiality extend across roles. Before sharing information, confirm who holds educational decision-making authority and, if required, obtain written, targeted releases that specify what may be disclosed and to whom. Apply a minimum-necessary standard and limit discussion to facts that inform referral, evaluation, services, safety, or compliance with court orders. Furthermore, consider being additive, rather than superfluous, in your discussion. If something has been said and it's true, you need not add more; however, if something is said and it is incorrect, it is appropriate to speak up. Critically, child welfare workers must not disclose protected case materials unless explicitly authorized. When uncertainty arises, pause, consult your supervisor, and defer disclosure until authority is clear. After any exchange, it is good practice to record what was shared, with whom, and the purpose for the disclosure.

Sarah meets with Alex's grandmother at her home. She shares what she has learned about the participants at the upcoming IEP meeting. Ms. Jones is grateful. She again reiterates that she's never attended an IEP meeting before, but explains that she knows there are many legal rights afforded to parents to make educational decisions. Still, she wonders, since she has not yet legally adopted Alex, what rights she has to make this decision formally. Sarah, once again, has a similar question.

How Is Your Role in the Special Education Process Different from That of a Parent?

Confusion about who is legally allowed to serve as a parent in formal meetings, such as IEPs, is not unwarranted. The definition is filled with nuances. Legally, a parent is defined as:

> (1) A biological or adoptive parent of a child; (2) A foster parent, unless State law, regulations, or contractual obligations with a State or local entity prohibit a foster parent from acting as a parent; (3) A guardian generally authorized to act as the child's parent, or authorized to make educational decisions for the child (but not the State if the child is a ward of the State); (4) An individual acting in the place of a biological or adoptive parent (including a grandparent, stepparent, or other relative) with whom the child lives, or an individual who is legally responsible for the child's welfare; or (5) A surrogate parent who has been appointed in accordance with § 300.519 or section 639(a)(5) of the Act. (34 C.F.R. § 300.30)

If a biological or adoptive parent retains educational rights and wishes to participate, then they maintain the right to participate in the IEP meeting in the role of parent. Importantly, this includes parents whose children may have been removed from their care and are in foster care. If Alex's mother retained her parental rights, then she would serve in the role of parent at the IEP meeting. In our vignette, she voluntarily terminated her parental rights; however, parental rights can be terminated by the court if it finds grounds for termination and follows the appropriate procedures. Considering its seriousness, the termination process can take years, and the grounds for terminating parental rights vary from state to state. For children who are wards of the state or court, meaning they have no parent acting in a legal capacity, a foster parent or legal guardian can serve in this role at an IEP meeting. Additionally, a surrogate parent can be appointed by a public agency. However, a foster care social worker or agency representative cannot serve as a surrogate parent and does not have formal educational rights. Surrogate parents must (a) not be employed by the local education agency or school, (b) have no personal interests that conflict with the best interests of the child, and (c) have knowledge and skills that ensure adequate representation of the child (34 C.F.R. § 300.519 [f]). The exact procedures for appointing a surrogate parent or educational representation vary from state to state and, in many cases, county to county. As such, before beginning any communication with school staff about the educational needs or the progress of children in care, verify who in the child's life has educational rights. This task can often be completed by checking with the court, child welfare agency, or your supervisor.

It is crucial to remember that parents and caregivers play a significant role in making decisions related to their children's educational welfare. Considering the upheaval brought about by the removal of children, decisions about who has or does not have educational rights can become very contentious. When collaborating to meet a child's academic needs, it is essential to respect the rights of parents and caregivers. After all, they can offer a unique perspective that benefits the development of comprehensive IEPs.

The Perspective of Parents and Caregivers

Whether a biological, adoptive parent, or guardian, most long-term caregivers bring an intimate knowledge of their child's history, strengths, preferences, and needs to the IEP process. They serve as the primary advocates for their children and have a vested interest in ensuring that their educational needs are met. Parents often face emotional connections to their child's academic journey, which may drive them to participate actively in meetings, voice their concerns, and advocate for their child's rights. Their input is crucial in elaborating on the child's developmental history, previous educational experiences, and family dynamics that may influence learning.

However, parents may also encounter challenges in navigating the complexities of special education (Gershwin et al., 2022). Many may not be familiar with legal frameworks, educational jargon, or procedural requirements. Their emotional investment can lead to stress or anxiety, particularly if they feel that their child's needs are not being adequately addressed. It is not uncommon for parents to feel overwhelmed by the system, which can lead to frustration and challenges in communicating with school personnel. Despite these challenges, parents' emotional investment and deep understanding of their children make them invaluable participants in the IEP process. Their perspective allows for a more personalized approach to the education plan, ensuring that it is aligned with the child's interests and aspirations.

The Unique Role of a Child Welfare Worker

As a child welfare worker, your role is to advocate for the child's overall well-being while supporting the educational goals outlined in the Individualized Education Program (IEP). Your role in special education meetings may vary depending on your specific job. For example, a foster parent may have education rights, while a CASA may serve a less direct role. Even so, as a child welfare worker, you approach the situation with a broader perspective that encompasses not only academic needs but also social, emotional, and environmental factors that impact the child's development. Your position uniquely enables you to serve as a bridge between the school team and other systems that influence the child's life. This role can include responsibilities such as coordinating with service providers, including mental health providers and community organizations. Additionally, your experience in dealing with families in crisis allows you to understand the broader context in which the child is operating, providing insights that other team members may not have. Compared to parents, while you focus on the child's unique needs, as a child welfare worker, you also need to consider systemic factors affecting education and what external support may be required. Your advocacy often extends beyond just ensuring compliance with educational legalities; it also involves coordinating resources and support services that may be necessary for a holistic approach to the child's education and well-being while maintaining confidentiality.

Both Sarah and Ms. Jones feel more comfortable attending the upcoming meeting. They both understand their roles and who else will be in attendance. In preparation, they review Alex's most recent IEP goals and progress reports. They take notes of questions they have and highlight grades and written feedback from teachers. Progress toward meeting reading goals concerns both women. Alex is three grade levels behind in reading and, despite three hours a week of intensive intervention, has not made adequate progress. They agree that advocating for an increase in service hours with a reading specialist is necessary to demonstrate sufficient progress toward IEP goals. Ms. Jones is enthusiastic about the possibility of getting more services. Sarah, on the other hand, understands that they might receive pushback from the school team. Sarah has heard from other CASAs that schools in their district, facing a critical shortage of reading specialists, are reluctant to add more service hours to their students' IEPs. Sarah shares with Ms. Jones that they will have to advocate for an increase in service hours by effectively communicating Alex's needs.

What Are Some Best Practices in Collaboration?

Ensuring effective collaboration among all participants in the special education process is critical to developing a well-rounded IEP that meets the child's individual needs (CADRE, 2022). Implementing the following practices can help facilitate effective communication, strengthen partnerships, and ultimately lead to better outcomes for the child.

Open and Regular Communication

Open and regular communication is paramount in establishing trust and transparency among team members. Ideally, there should be a relationship built among the IEP team members before any meetings. The school team, including teachers, related service providers, and administrators as needed, should maintain regular contact, sharing progress toward IEP goals and any notable concerns. Parents, caregivers, and child welfare workers should also proactively reach out to the school team as needed to share concerns and monitor progress. Communication should occur both ways to ensure that everyone is informed about the child's progress and that there are no surprises when the IEP meeting takes place—using straightforward language to minimize misunderstandings and encourage participants to express their thoughts and concerns.

Sarah suggested they begin by proactively initiating communication before the formal meeting. She proposed sending a concise email to the IEP team, including the special education teacher, general education teacher, school psychologist, and administrator, outlining their primary concerns regarding Alex's reading progress and formally requesting the increase in services. This preemptive communication strategy not only established their priorities but also opened a productive dialogue several days in advance of the meeting.

Active Listening and Perspective-Taking

Active listening is essential in collaboration. Each member of the IEP team should be encouraged to listen attentively and consider the perspectives of others without interrupting. This practice creates an inclusive environment where everyone feels valued. Table 4.1 provides examples and non-examples of collaborative language to use during meetings. Just as each participant has a unique role, their perspectives are also shaped by personal views, job requirements, and professional knowledge. Sometimes, these perspectives can conflict. Perspective-taking often involves recognizing the expertise that each member brings to the table. Each participant has unique knowledge, skills, and expertise, whether it be the special education teacher's instructional strategies, the psychologist's assessment techniques, or the parents' understanding of their child. Furthermore, listening to understand rather than listening to respond will help every team member feel heard and will lessen the chance that words or motives are misconstrued (see Brownlee, 2020). After all, every team member should be working toward shared goals.

During the meeting, the school team began by setting meeting norms, emphasizing the importance of active listening—attentively hearing each participant's perspective without interruption. Sarah encouraged Ms. Jones to actively note the team members' responses and any nonverbal cues that might suggest their viewpoints or concerns. To prepare for this, they had spent the previous day discussing how they anticipated each team member might react to their request for additional support. They also practiced articulating their points while anticipating possible pushback and brainstorming suitable responses.

Setting Shared Goals

The IEP team should work collaboratively to create a shared vision for the child's educational goals. Establishing common objectives focuses everyone's efforts on supporting the child's best interests and ensures that all members are committed to achieving those goals. Using the SMART criteria for goals—Specific, Measurable, Achievable, Relevant, and Time-bound—can facilitate clear, actionable targets that everyone can rally around. Goals are a formal process in the IEP and will be discussed in the next chapter.

Sarah and Ms. Jones clearly articulate the shared goals: keeping Alex at his current school, seeing him make significant progress in reading, and addressing his behavioral challenges. They agreed to reiterate these goals at the start of the meeting, ensuring everyone understood their priorities and vision. The school team agreed wholeheartedly with these goals.

Flexibility and Patience

Flexibility is key in the collaborative process, as participants may have differing viewpoints and experiences. Though special education may seem laden with compliance requirements, educating children is anything but a cut-and-dry endeavor. Unfortunately, plans change, people are absent, meetings get canceled, and children (and adults) behave poorly at times. Recognizing that adjustments may be necessary as new information becomes available is an important component of being an effective communicator during special education meetings. Having your priorities in mind when entering a meeting helps you clearly identify non-negotiables and areas where flexibility is possible. Similarly, practicing patience allows team members to navigate disagreements respectfully and constructively, ultimately achieving a collaborative effort that puts the child's needs first.

Table 4.1 Collaborative Language: Dos and Don'ts

Do Say	Don't Say
"I appreciate your perspective on this."	"That's not how we do things here."
"Can you provide an example?"	"I don't see the relevance."
"Let's explore that further together."	"There's no point in discussing this."
"I see how this could be important to you."	"This isn't a priority right now."
"What other supports might be beneficial?"	"We can't do that."
"This is a helpful point, thank you for raising it."	"We've never done that before."
"Could you help me understand this better?"	"I don't understand what you're saying."
"What has worked well in the past?"	"That's not my job."
"How can we ensure this aligns with our goals?"	"We don't have time for this."
"I would like to hear more about your concerns."	"Let's move on; this isn't important."
"What are your thoughts on this suggestion?"	"I disagree with you."
"It's valuable to hear your insights."	"This is the only way to do it."
"Let's ensure we're on the same page."	"There's no need to discuss this any further."
"Thank you for bringing that to our attention."	"I'm not interested in this right now."
"How can we address these challenges together?"	"That's not possible."
"What outcomes are you hoping to see?"	"You're being unrealistic."
"Can you elaborate on that point?"	"I don't think that's relevant."
"How does this align with your expectations?"	"I can't help with that."
"It's important to consider all perspectives."	"Your input isn't needed here."
"Let's summarize what we've discussed so far."	"I've already made a decision."

While increased reading support remained non-negotiable, Sarah advised Ms. Jones to stay flexible. If immediate additional hours were not feasible, they agreed to explore alternative strategies, such as tutoring, additional classroom support, or a modified approach to intensive intervention. They planned to discuss available resources and compromises with the team, patiently addressing any objections with thoughtful, evidence-based counterarguments.

Conflict Resolution

Conflict can arise during collaboration when differing viewpoints clash or when misunderstandings occur. Emotions can be heightened during IEP meetings. Establishing clear procedures for conflict resolution is essential. Taking a break, reiterating the shared goals, and seeking areas of agreement or compromise can be helpful in finding consensus. Identifying a neutral party to mediate discussions can also be successful in resolving disagreements. The procedures of mediation and dispute resolution are discussed in Chapter 10, along with other strategies for reaching a consensus. During IEP meetings, addressing conflict openly and respectfully ensures that it does not hinder the overall collaborative process and allows for constructive solutions that benefit the child. Employing active listening skills and perspective-taking are critical components of conflict resolution.

In the event of conflict or pushback, Sarah suggests a collaborative approach, emphasizing areas of common ground before addressing disagreements. They would frame their requests around Alex's specific needs and present data they have compiled demonstrating the current intervention's inadequacy. They agreed to express any concerns calmly and respectfully, acknowledging any support already offered by the school while making it clear that further intervention was essential. Sarah and Ms. Jones also prepared for the potential need to suggest a structured mediation process if the initial discussion became unproductive.

Following Up

Following up regularly after meetings allows you to assess whether the agreed-upon goals and strategies are being implemented and can help ensure accountability and reinforce progress toward achieving shared objectives. Establishing a timeline for regular check-ins can structure this process, allowing the team to discuss what is working for the child, what is not, and what may need to be adjusted to improve the IEP. The IEP meeting should not be the first or last time the team hears from you.

The school team acknowledged Sarah and Ms. Jones' concerns. They agreed that additional support in a resource room was appropriate to meet Alex's reading needs. Additionally, they were thankful to get to brainstorm with Ms. Jones' about preferred positive reinforcement activities they can try with Alex to increase his time on task and decrease behaviors of concern. Sarah, Ms. Jones, and the rest of the IEP team reinforced the importance of consistent communication after the meeting. Ms. Jones planned a follow-up email thanking the team for their time and effort, reiterating their main points, and ensuring that the school team understands she is available for subsequent meetings as needed to discuss Alex's progress.

As a child welfare worker, your role is integral to the collaborative success of special education. You uniquely assist caregivers by navigating complex systems and provide school teams with essential contextual information about a child's history and needs. Effective special education relies on collaboration to ensure that students with disabilities receive comprehensive, individualized support. This outcome requires the active involvement of educators, families, related service providers, and other stakeholders. Your collaboration should extend beyond IEP meetings and include proactive communication at key times, such as when new cases start, the new school year begins, or changes occur to school or placement. The next chapter delves deeply into IEP structure and development, referencing the six key components of IDEA and the "gears of special education" framework.

Where Can I Find More Information About Collaboration in Special Education?

- **Module:** *IRIS Center—Collaborating with Families of Students with Disabilities*

  The IRIS Center at Vanderbilt University offers helpful modules that explain the essential elements of special education. Check out their module on strategies to collaborate with families of students with disabilities: https://iris.peabody.vanderbilt.edu/module/fam/

- **Website:** *The Center for Appropriate Dispute Resolution in Special Education (CADRE)*

  CADRE creates and disseminates various resources, including manuals, guides, and model policies, to enhance dispute-resolution practices and facilitate consensus-building. Take a look at their resources here: https://www.cadreworks.org/resources

- **Website:** *Virginia Commonwealth University's Resources for Creating Collaborative IEPs*

  These resources, particularly in session one, highlight strategies for working collaboratively throughout the IEP process. See downloadable handouts here: https://partnership.vcu.edu/resources/creating-collaborative-ieps/

- **Database:** *Child Welfare Information Gateway (CWIG)*

  The CWIG is a service of the US Children's Bureau. It provides resources and information on various aspects of child welfare, including interagency collaboration, working with families, and trauma-informed care. https://www.childwelfare.gov/resources/library-catalog/

References

Brownlee, D. (2020, August 6). Are you really listening, or just waiting to talk? There's a difference. *Forbes*. https://www.forbes.com/sites/danabrownlee/2020/08/06/are-you-really-listening-or-just-waiting-to-talk-theres-a-difference/

Center for Appropriate Dispute Resolution in Special Education (CADRE). (2022). *Collaborative advocacy guiding principles*. https://www.cadreworks.org/media/6633/download?attachment

Gershwin, T., McKittrick, L., & Kilpatrick, A. (2022). The importance of following legal requirements: Factors that lead to parent satisfaction with the individualized education program meeting process. *Journal*

of Educational and Psychological Consultation. https://doi.org/10.1080/10474412.2022.2145290
Individuals with Disabilities Education Act of 2004, 20 U.S.C. § 1400.

5

Individualized Education Programs (IEPs) and 504 Plans

The Individuals with Disabilities Education Act (IDEA, 2004) established the gears of special education. The law enshrines a free appropriate public education (FAPE) for students with disabilities through an individualized education program (IEP). IDEA is not the only federal legislation that protects children with disabilities. Anti-discrimination advocacy led the federal government to pass another significant piece of legislation concerning the rights of all people with disabilities. The Rehabilitation Act of 1973 was the first major legislative attempt to prohibit discrimination on the basis of disability. There are several sections to the Act; however, in terms of education and schools, Section 504 of the Rehabilitation Act is most relevant. Simply called Section 504, this part of the law prohibits discrimination against qualified individuals with disabilities by any program or activity receiving federal financial assistance. Since nearly all public schools receive federal funding, Section 504 applies to public K-12 schools.

As a child welfare worker who will likely care for a child with a disability and interact with school personnel, it is imperative that you have the confidence to serve on an IEP team and advocate for your child. Knowing how to contribute to the development of a 504 Plan or IEP might make a meaningful difference in the child's accommodations and academic success. In this chapter, we will use a fictional vignette to explore the process of special education and answer the following questions about IEPs and 504 Plans:

1. What are the differences between IEPs and 504 Plans?
2. How does a student qualify for special education services?
3. What are the main components of an IEP?
4. How can I contribute to the development of a high-quality IEP?
5. Where can I find more information about IEPs and 504 Plans?

Ms. Taylor recently completed her training to become a Court Appointed Special Advocate (CASA). She had been thinking about becoming a CASA volunteer for many years. Still, as an executive at a local nonprofit organization, the intensive training and time commitment prevented her from taking the leap. Now that she has finished the training and is about to get her first case, she is excited! Ms. Taylor meets her supervisor in the CASA office to review a couple of open cases that need a CASA volunteer. After reviewing the files, she selects a case about a 7-year-old girl named Mia, who has been placed in the care of a relative. The order adjudicating Mia as a child in need of services states that Mia, who is in first grade, has been absent for more than 20 days in the current school year. Mia did not attend kindergarten the previous year. When child protective services (CPS) performed a well-being check after the school reported chronic absenteeism, they found the house to be in extreme disarray with no electricity and heat. The home was deemed unlivable due to sanitary conditions and a lack of basic necessities. Mia was relocated to her maternal aunt's house in a nearby town. Ms. Taylor begins doing her homework to find out more about Mia's home and school history. She wants to have enough background knowledge before she meets Mia and the school personnel.

What Are the Differences Between IEPs and 504 Plans?

Two laws protect children with disabilities and provide them with additional support and services in schools. IDEA is an educational law regulated by the Department of Education, while Section 504 is a civil rights (anti-discrimination) law under the Department of Health and Human Services. Both laws declare that students with disabilities are entitled to FAPE; however, the differences in definitions of FAPE between the laws are critically important. As was discussed in Chapter 3, FAPE per IDEA is about following the procedures of the law and providing a reasonably calculated IEP to enable the student to make appropriate progress in light of the student's circumstances. Under IDEA, FAPE is about equity in education, meaning that students with disabilities are provided with supports and services to achieve an equal educational opportunity. Under Section 504, FAPE is a term of equivalence, meaning students with disabilities must be afforded a comparable education to their nondisabled peers with necessary accommodations and services to remove barriers to learning.

To qualify for protections under Section 504, the law defines disability as:

> Any person who (a) has a physical or mental impairment which substantially limits one or more of such person's major life activities, (b) has a record of such an impairment, or (c) is regarded as having such an impairment.

Table 5.1 presents differences between IDEA and Section 504. Under IDEA, students can only qualify for special education if they are diagnosed within the thirteen disability categories, and that disability negatively impacts their educational progress. The definition of disability under Section 504 is broader, meaning more students may qualify for accommodations under Section 504 than under IDEA. Furthermore, the Office of Civil Rights in the Department of Education monitors compliance with and enforces provisions of Section 504. In contrast, state education agencies and the Office of Special Education Programs enforce IDEA. The level of services provided under IDEA is also more extensive.

Special education, developed and delivered through the IEP, is designed to provide specially designed instruction (SDI) to help students work toward their IEP goals. Accommodations and modifications are often provided to accomplish this task. Child welfare workers should be aware of the distinction between these two terms. *Accommodations* help students with disabilities learn the same material as their nondisabled peers in a different way. Accommodations change *how* the student learns—for example, extra time on tests, preferential seating, frequent breaks, or shorter assignments. The student is still learning the same material; however, the way they learn has been accommodated. *Modifications* are adjustments to the curriculum or expectations. Modifications change

Table 5.1 Differences Between IDEA and Section 504

	IDEA	Section 504
Purpose	Ensures that children with disabilities receive a free appropriate public education (FAPE) tailored to their individual needs.	Prohibits discrimination on the basis of disability in programs and activities that receive federal financial assistance.
Eligibility	Students must have one of thirteen specified disabilities that significantly impact their educational performance.	Students must have a physical or mental impairment that substantially limits one or more major life activities.
Services	Provides a wide range of specialized educational and related services, such as specially designed instruction, speech therapy, and occupational therapy.	Requires schools to provide reasonable accommodations to ensure equal access to education, such as extended time on tests, preferential seating, or assistive technology.
Legal Protections	Offers extensive procedural safeguards, including the right to an Individualized Education Program (IEP), parental involvement, and due process.	Provides fewer procedural safeguards than IDEA but ensures access to education with a 504 Plan.

what the student learns—for example, alternative assignments, modified textbooks, different grading scales, or learning different content.

Under Section 504, students with disabilities are only offered accommodations to access the general education curriculum. If a student's disability is significantly impacting their educational progress, they will likely qualify for special education and receive accommodations and modifications to help them progress toward their individual goals. An example of a student who might benefit from a 504 Plan is a student who has a respiratory condition. The student's 504 Plan might allow frequent visits to the nurse's office to use their medicated inhaler as needed. The 504 Plan might also state that limited physical activity during physical education is approved, given the student's respiratory needs. These are accommodations that allow the student to participate and have a "comparable" education to their nondisabled peers. A 504 Plan allows all school personnel to be aware of and adhere to reasonable accommodations.

Ms. Taylor meets Mia for the first time and finds out that she is a very sweet girl. Of course, Mia is hesitant to talk to a stranger at first, given the major changes in her life, but after a few minutes, she shows Ms. Taylor her new room and toys. She also warms up when she shows Ms. Taylor the friendly family cat that Mia is now proudly responsible for feeding.

After speaking with Mia's aunt and teachers at her previous school and current school, it is evident that Mia is academically far behind her peers. Mia recognizes only a few alphabet letters, and she is unable to blend beginning words like "cat" or "red." Ms. Taylor and school personnel discuss whether Mia should be evaluated for special education services.

How Does a Student Qualify for Special Education Services?

For a student to become eligible for special education, they must undergo a comprehensive evaluation. The evaluation will identify specific needs of the student and clarify whether those needs require special education services. The process may seem long, but it ensures that only students who actually need special education receive services. The evaluation process also ensures that students without disabilities are not placed in special education because they had a couple of bad days in the classroom. There are multiple checks and balances in the system to confirm that a nondiscriminatory evaluation takes place. Nondiscriminatory means that the evaluation process is not biased in favor of or against any individual or group of students (Markelz & Bateman, 2022).

"Child find" is an important legal component of IDEA. It puts an affirmative duty on states and school districts to seek out and identify children with disabilities proactively. State government and school personnel cannot sit back and wait for children with disabilities to be referred for evaluations. School personnel, a parent, or a state agency can initiate a request for an evaluation. Once a written request for an evaluation has been received by school personnel, a multidisciplinary team meets to review preliminary data, such as student grades, behaviors, and coursework assignments, to determine if an evaluation is warranted. Suppose the multidisciplinary team believes that an evaluation is required to determine whether the student has a disability that is negatively impacting their education. In that case, the team must document the consent of the parent or legal guardian to perform the evaluation. According to IDEA, a school has 60 business days to complete an evaluation after receiving consent. Some states have shorter procedural requirements, such as Indiana, which requires an evaluation within 50 business days.

In the past, school districts relied on evaluation assessments that were racially and culturally biased. In particular, intelligence quotient (IQ) assessments were standardized with populations of students that were not demographically representative of all students. Discriminatory evaluations became a particular concern in special education due to the overrepresentation of minority students or students from economically disadvantaged backgrounds (Yell, 2019). Schools were solely relying on IQ assessments to make special education eligibility decisions. To remedy this practice, IDEA was amended in 2004 to enhance the rules and procedures for conducting nondiscriminatory evaluations. Figure 5.1 presents three key procedural and substantive components of a nondiscriminatory evaluation (Markelz & Bateman, 2022).

Response to Intervention (RTI)

A variety of valid assessments have been developed over the years to identify qualifying disabilities under IDEA. If you recall from Chapter 2, the category of specific learning disability (SLD) is the largest percentage (32 percent) of students receiving special education services (The National Center for Education Statistics, 2024). This category has a unique identification procedure and should be familiar to child welfare workers.

Prior to 2004, schools used the "discrepancy model" to determine whether a student had a specific learning disability by comparing the student's intellectual ability and academic achievement (Murawski & Scott, 2017). If the student's IQ indicated average intelligence (between 85 and 115), yet the student was academically performing significantly below their age-appropriate peers, a discrepancy was noted, and the student may qualify for special education services. Many critiques of the discrepancy model have emerged since it was codified in law in 1977 (US Office of Education, 1977). The most common critique was that the deficit model of identification led to a wait-to-fail approach to identifying disability and providing special

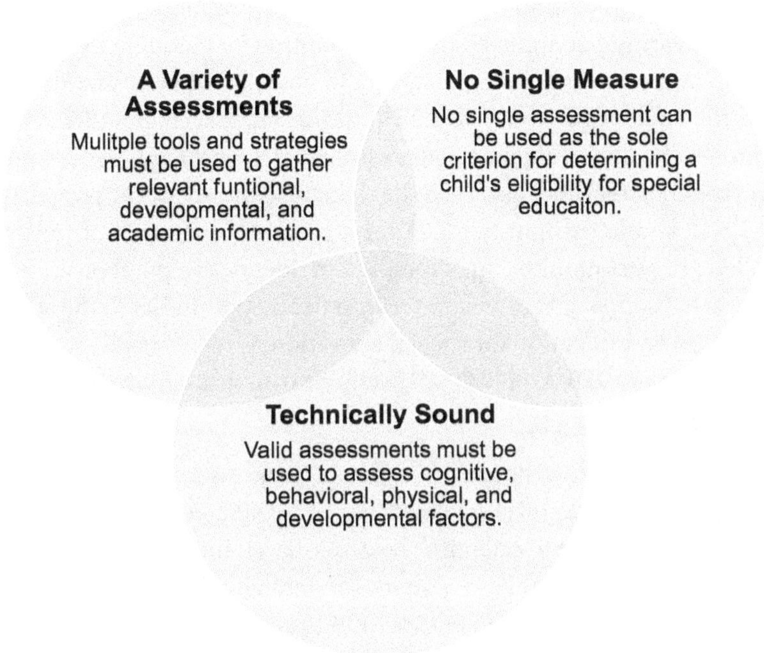

Figure 5.1. Venn diagram of the three components to a nondiscriminatory evaluation.

education services (Kavale & Flanagan, 2007). The discrepancy between a student's IQ and achievement could not be identified until a substantial amount of time had passed. A student was therefore required to struggle academically for a long enough period until a significant deficit developed between their IQ and academic ability. Often, this meant a student would struggle academically for years until they qualified for special education services (Markelz & Bateman, 2022).

In 2004, IDEA was amended with the following criteria for determining whether a child has a specific learning disability:

- States must not require the use of a severe discrepancy between intellectual ability and achievement for determining whether a child has a specific learning disability;
- States must permit the use of a process based on the child's response to scientific, research-based intervention; and
- States may permit the use of other alternative research-based procedures for determining whether a child has a specific learning disability.

Response to Intervention (RTI) has become the new model for identifying a specific learning disability. Rather than waiting for a student to fail, levels of academic support are systematically increased and then monitored to see if the student responds positively to the support. Figure 5.2 visually represents the tiers of support that are provided in an RTI model. A student who does not respond positively to the academic supports provided in tier 1 will be moved into tier 2. After a reasonable amount of time and detailed progress monitoring, if the student does not respond positively to the targeted support, they will move into tier 3. Within tier 3, the student will receive an evaluation for special education.

According to IDEA (2004), a specific learning disability diagnosis is determined by:

- The student does not make sufficient progress to meet age or state-approved grade-level standards when using a process based on the child's response to scientific, research-based intervention; or
- The student exhibits a pattern of strengths and weaknesses in performance, achievement, or both, relative to age or intellectual development, that is determined by the group to be relevant to the identification of a specific learning disability, using appropriate assessments, and is not primarily the result of:
  - A visual, hearing, or motor disability
  - Intellectual disability
  - Emotional disturbance
  - Cultural factors
  - Environmental or economic disadvantage
  - Limited English proficiency.

As you can see, the determination of a specific learning disability is also about eliminating other reasons for poor academic achievement. In addition, to ensure that underachievement in a student suspected of having a specific learning disability is not due to a lack of appropriate instruction in reading or math, the evaluation must demonstrate that prior to the evaluation, the student was provided with appropriate instruction in regular education settings, delivered by qualified personnel.

Suppose a child has chronic absenteeism, which is almost certain in educational neglect CPS cases. In that case, a school's multidisciplinary team might be hesitant to approve an evaluation of a child suspected of a

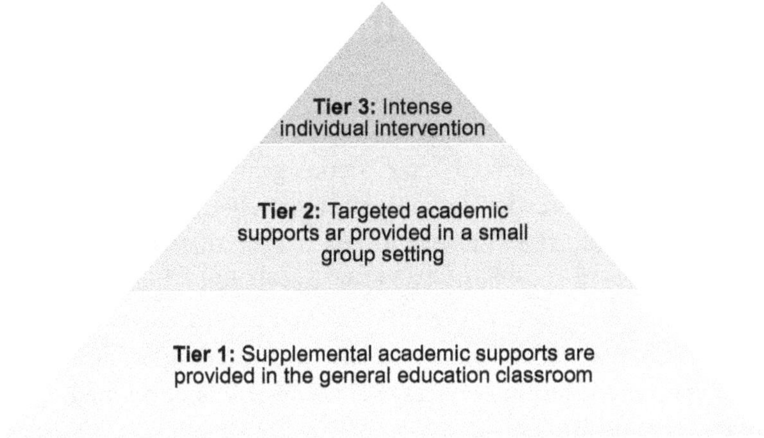

Figure 5.2. Levels of support within the response to intervention (RTI) model.

specific learning disability. It stands to reason that a child who is not in school cannot benefit from appropriate instruction. Therefore, the child's poor academic performance may be related to their absences, rather than to a disability. School personnel, however, understand the traumatic events leading to a child in need of protective services. If you and other adults in the child's life are concerned that the child might have a specific learning disability, then open communication with school personnel is needed. With a little persistence and advocacy as the child's welfare worker, the school will likely agree to an expedited RTI process or initiate the evaluation process, knowing that absenteeism is a variable to consider when making an eligibility determination.

Ms. Taylor and Mia's aunt believe Mia's low academic abilities are not related to a lack of instruction. They suspect Mia's difficult home life, which consisted of neglect and malnutrition, may have contributed to a developmental delay. They both sign a letter asking Mia's new school to conduct an evaluation to determine if she has a disability and if that disability is negatively impacting her educational progress. The multidisciplinary team agrees that an evaluation of Mia is warranted and begins the nondiscriminatory evaluation process. Twenty-five days later, the school psychologist has completed Mia's evaluation. It is determined that Mia qualifies for special education as a student with an intellectual disability. The next step is for the team to meet, discuss the results of the evaluation, and develop an IEP for Mia.

What Are the Main Components of an IEP?

As you may recall from Chapter 3, the gears of special education work together to procedurally and substantively define FAPE for each individual student. The IEP is the largest gear that drives the whole process because it is where FAPE is developed, documented, and delivered (Bateman, 2017). The IEP is a legal contract signed by school personnel and parents or legal guardians, documenting the agreed-upon plan of special education services. Before an IEP is developed, the IEP team needs to be formed.

IDEA (2004) identifies those who are required to be on an IEP team as well as those who are permitted but not required. The IEP team members who are required are: (a) the student's parents or legal guardians, (b) at least one special education teacher, (c) at least one general education teacher, (d) a representative from the local educational agency that is qualified to provide or supervise the special education program (usually the school principal), and (e) the child, when appropriate (required for a transition IEP). IEP team members who are permitted but not required are those who bring additional expertise to the team, depending on the student's individual needs, such as a child welfare worker, an assistive technology expert, or a related service provider.

Developing an IEP requires the IEP team to address eight main components (see Table 5.2). These eight components combine to create the product, or written document, of a student's IEP. To start, a student's present levels of academic achievement and functional performance (PLAAFP) must be assessed and stated in the IEP. As was discussed in Chapter 3, the PLAAFP statement is a result of the nondiscriminatory evaluation and substantively contributes to FAPE by defining the "student's circumstance." Only after the student's circumstances are identified can the team develop goals and objectives.

The second component of an IEP is determining measurable annual goals and short-term objectives. In other words, where does the IEP team want the student to be academically and functionally in one year? The annual goal establishes a final target, while short-term objectives allow the IEP team to track the student's progress along the way. Substantial research has explored the quality of IEP goals and objectives, with a general consensus identifying specific, measurable, attainable, relevant, and time-bound (SMART) goals as the most effective (Hedin & DeSpain, 2018).

After SMART IEP goals have been developed, the IEP team must identify how the student's progress toward meeting those goals will be measured and when progress will be reported to the student's parents. Regular progress monitoring is critical because (a) it keeps parents/legal guardians involved as collaborating participants in the child's education, and (b) it allows the IEP team to collect, analyze, and report data to determine if the special education supports are working as intended or not. Suppose the student is making adequate progress toward their annual goal and meeting short-term objectives; then great! The IEP team can continue as planned. If, however, the student is not making adequate progress as outlined by short-term objectives, then the IEP team should meet and discuss necessary support and service changes to provide greater

Table 5.2 Main Components of an IEP

1. A statement of the student's present levels of academic achievement and functional performance.
2. A statement of the student's measurable annual goals and short-term objectives.
3. A statement of how the student's progress toward meeting those goals will be measured and when progress will be reported to the student's parents.
4. A statement of the special education, related services, and supplemental aids and services that will be provided to the student.
5. An examination and statement of the extent to which the student will not participate in the general education classroom.
6. A statement of necessary accommodations for the student to participate in statewide academic assessments; or a statement of how an alternative assessment was selected.
7. A statement of measurable post-secondary goals based on age-appropriate transition services (must be included for students who are 16 years old or older; state laws may requiretransition goals for students 14 or 15 years old or older).
8. The projected date for beginning special education services and the anticipated duration of the IEP.

educational benefit. Systematic progress monitoring is an essential substantive requirement that shows a data-based, data-driven IEP is reasonably calculated to enable the student to make progress appropriate in light of their circumstances.

After the goals are stated, the IEP team must determine the special education services, related services, and supplemental aids and services that will be provided to the student. Each need identified in the student's PLAAFP must be addressed by one of these services. Solely, or in combination, the services identified in this section of the IEP are the actions the school will take to enable the student to make progress in light of their circumstances. It is important to know the difference between these three types of services.

Special Education Services

A student who requires special education services should be provided with specially designed instruction (SDI). SDI is defined as:

> Adapting, as appropriate to the needs of an eligible child, the content, methodology, or delivery of instruction to address the unique needs of the child that result from the child's disability and to ensure access of the child to the general curriculum, so that the child can meet the educational standards within the jurisdiction of the public agency that apply to all children. (34 C.F.R. § 300.39[b][3])

Related Services

Related services allow a student to benefit from special education. Federal IDEA regulations (2012) define related services as:

> Supportive services [. . .] [including] speech-language pathology and audiology services, interpreting services, psychological services, physical and occupational therapy, recreation, including therapeutic recreation, early identification and assessment of disabilities in children, counseling services, including rehabilitation counseling, orientation and mobility services, and medical services for diagnostic or evaluation purposes. Related services also include school health services and school nurse services, social work services in schools, and parent counseling and training. (34 C.F.R. § 300.34[a])

Supplemental Aids and Services

Supplemental aids and services are "aids, services, and other supports that are provided in regular classes, other education-related settings, and in extracurricular and non-academic settings, to enable students with disabilities to be educated with students without disabilities to the maximum extent appropriate" (34 C.F.R. § 300.42). Examples of supplemental aids and services may involve special seating arrangements for the student, using professional or student tutors, or working with the student's parents to help the child at home.

After a student's goals are drafted and services to meet those goals are identified, the IEP team must determine the student's least restrictive environment (LRE) to receive those services. In doing so, the IEP team decides the extent to which the student *will not* participate in the general education classroom. A student's LRE can only be determined on an individual, case-by-case basis because each student's PLAAFP, goals, and services are unique. The IEP team must remember that IDEA (2004) requires students with disabilities to be educated alongside children without disabilities to the *maximum extent appropriate*. FAPE and LRE must be considered together, taking into account the student's goals and circumstances.

The sixth substantive component of the IEP is a statement of necessary accommodations for the student to participate in statewide academic assessments, or a statement explaining how an alternative assessment was selected. A result of the No Child Left Behind Act (2001) and the Every Student Succeeds Act (2015) was that students with disabilities were also included in school accountability assessments. States provide a list of accommodations to assist students with disabilities who are administered state academic assessments (e.g., extended time, testing in a separate location). For students with more severe disabilities, however, states are required to provide an alternative assessment that is based on modified or alternative academic standards.

If a student is old enough (sixteen or older), their IEP must include a statement of measurable post-secondary goals based on age-appropriate transition services. Some state laws require transition goals for students as young as thirteen years old. Post-secondary goals and transition services help students and their families prepare for life after school. The purpose of including transition services several years before a student ages out of

IDEA protections is to (a) create a longer-term outlook into the IEP process; (b) assist each student in making a meaningful transition from the school setting to a post-school setting, which could include higher education, employment, or independent living; and (c) help students better reach their potential as adults. Chapter 9 explores the process of post-secondary transition in detail.

Lastly, an IEP must include the projected date for beginning special education services and the anticipated duration of the IEP. The IEP must be implemented as soon as possible after it is written. In terms of duration, the IEP must be reviewed at least once a year (Office of Special Education Programs, 2000).

Over the past several weeks, Ms. Taylor has been developing a relationship with Mia and learning about her history from Mia's aunt, her teachers, and Mia's CPS case manager. The school has set a date for the IEP team to meet and develop Mia's Individualized Education Program (IEP). Since Ms. Taylor lacks experience with special education procedures, she wants to be prepared for the meeting. She wants to advocate for Mia's interests, and to do so at an IEP meeting, she must be knowledgeable and comfortable with what to expect.

How Can I Contribute to the Development of a High-Quality IEP?

Special education, like most fields of knowledge, has technical jargon, complex concepts, and numerous acronyms (e.g., LRE, SDI, IDEA, IEP, FAPE, and many more). As a child welfare worker who has not been exposed to the field of special education or worked with children having disabilities, an IEP meeting may seem daunting. You may feel hesitant to speak up or ask questions, sitting around a table of school personnel who might have had years of training and experience in special education. In Chapter 4, we discussed the roles of participants at an IEP meeting. We also discussed your role as a child welfare worker and presented some best practices for collaborating with IEP team members for the benefit of the child.

To help prepare for an initial IEP meeting, we provide Table 5.3. This checklist will help ensure the main components of the IEP are thoroughly discussed and that your input is heard and incorporated into the IEP. Similarly, Figure 5.3 highlights some pitfalls to avoid as you participate in crafting high-quality IEPs. As an advocate for the child and a critical member of the IEP team, your contribution directly relates to the substantive development of a Free and Appropriate Public Education (FAPE).

Before Mia's IEP meeting, Ms. Taylor conducts some additional research online about IEPs to familiarize herself with the document and the process. She reviews Mia's evaluation documents and writes down any questions she has. During the IEP meeting, Ms. Taylor is pleased to meet Mia's special education teacher and other administrators, who all express their desire to do what is best for Mia. The IEP team methodically works through the main components of the IEP in a collaborative manner. She feels like her questions are answered and her input is valued. Ms. Taylor hopes that Mia will find stability and support through receiving special education services and that her academic abilities will flourish.

Where Can I Find More Information About IEPs and 504 Plans?

- **Video:** *Elementary IEP Meeting*

  Searching YouTube will yield a variety of mock IEP meetings that can help familiarize you with the structure and flow of a typical IEP meeting. In particular, see https://youtu.be/MZw7IGRUMcA?si=n5MuOuoi9Y4F9HXn

- **Website:** *Understood.org*

  Understood.org provides many resources for parents of children with disabilities, including a page titled: *How to tell if your child's IEP goals are SMART?* https://www.understood.org/en/articles/how-to-tell-if-your-childs-iep-goals-are-smart

- **Book:** *Developing Educationally Meaningful and Legally Sound IEPs*

Table 5.3 Checklist for IEP Meeting Preparation

Items to Prepare Before the IEP Meeting	Yes	No
I have written down strengths I see in the child. Consider the whole child (academics, emotional, social, functional, communication).	☐	☐
I have written down areas of need I see in the child.	☐	☐
I have received a copy of the child's nondiscriminatory evaluation.	☐	☐
I have written down any questions I have about the evaluation results.	☐	☐
I am familiar with the eight components of an IEP.	☐	☐
Items to Check During the IEP Meeting	**Yes**	**No**
Does the PLAAFP statement describe the child accurately and comprehensively?	☐	☐
Does the PLAAFP statement include my input concerning the strengths/weakness of the child?	☐	☐
Are the annual goals specific, measurable, attainable, relevant, and time bound?	☐	☐
Based on the child's circumstances as written in the PLAAFP statement, I can describe "appropriate progress" toward their annual goals?	☐	☐
Was the general education classroom first considered as placement for special education services?	☐	☐
Did the IEP team consider placements down the continuum of services with the appropriateness of those placements in mind?	☐	☐
If the child is in a more restrictive environment, did the IEP team consider additional opportunities to be alongside their nondisabled peers?	☐	☐
Have all my questions been answered by the IEP team?	☐	☐

For a deeper dive into IEPs, this book addresses better practices in conducting assessments, developing PLAAFP statements, crafting measurable annual goals, determining special education services, and monitoring and reporting on students' progress.

- **Website:** *Department of Education*

  Section 504 Plans pertain to students with disabilities in K-12 schools. The US Department of Education has published a *Parent and Educator Resource Guide to Section 504 in Public Elementary and Secondary Schools.* This comprehensive resource provides a lot of information about Section 504. https://www.ed.gov/media/document/504-resource-guide-201612pdf

Confusing IEPs and 504 plans or missing eligibility options

Child welfare workers sometimes treat a 504 plan as a "lighter" IEP or assume that a student can easily move between the two. In reality, they arise from different laws, have different eligibility rules, and offer different levels of service. At the same time, teams may overlook Section 504 entirely if the child is not failing classes. This can result in a child receiving too little support or the wrong type of plan.

Focusing on diagnosis instead of educational impact and present levels

It is common to assume that a diagnosis automatically requires an IEP. Eligibility under IDEA depends on how the disability affects the child's access to and progress in school. When present levels of academic achievement and functional performance are incomplete or inaccurate, goals and services will not match the child's needs. A strong advocate connects history, trauma, current functioning, and school data to show how the disability affects learning and behavior.

Accepting vague or non-specific plans

IEPs and 504 plans sometimes include broad language such as "as needed," "extra help," or "when appropriate" without naming who will provide support, how often, or in what setting. Vague terms make accountability difficult. IEP team members can ask for clear, specific, and measurable descriptions of services, accommodations, and goals so everyone understands what is supposed to happen.

Staying silent about decisions and educational rights

Many child welfare workers feel outnumbered or unsure in meetings and hesitate to speak up. They may not be clear about who holds educational decision-making authority or whether they can sign documents. This can delay services or hide important concerns, such as the impact of multiple placements, school moves, or trauma. It is appropriate to ask questions, request examples, clarify who can sign, or pause a meeting to review documents.

Treating the plan as separate from the child welfare case and only acting in crisis

Educational supports are often viewed as separate from permanency planning, mental health treatment, and placement decisions. When systems are not coordinated, children may miss services or face conflicting expectations. Advocates sometimes wait until there is a crisis, such as failing classes or repeated suspensions, before requesting help and may not document concerns in writing. Early, written advocacy and regular review of implementation can prevent problems from escalating.

Figure 5.3. Common IEP pitfalls to avoid.

References

Bateman, B. D. (2017). Individualized education programs. In J. M. Kauffman and D. P. Hallahan (Eds.), *Handbook of special education* (2nd ed., pp. 91–124). Taylor & Francis/Routledge.

IDEA regulations, 34 C.F.R. § 300 (2012).

Individuals with Disabilities Education Act of 2004, 20 U.S.C. § 1400.

Hedin, L., & DeSpain, S. (2018). SMART or not? Writing specific, measurable IEP goals. *TEACHING Exceptional Children*, *51*(2), 100–110.

Kavale, K. A., & Flanagan, D. P. (2007). Ability—achievement discrepancy, response to intervention, and assessment of cognitive abilities/processes in specific learning disability identification: Toward a contemporary operational definition. In *Handbook of response to intervention* (pp. 130–147). Springer.

Markelz, A. M., & Bateman, D. F. (2022). *The essentials of special education law.* Rowman & Littlefield.

Murawski, W. W., & Scott, K. L. (2017). *What really works with exceptional learners.* Corwin Publishing.

National Center for Education Statistics. (2024). Students with disabilities. *Condition of Education.* U.S. Department of Education, Institute of Education Sciences. https://nces.ed.gov/programs/coe/indicator/cgg

Office of Special Education Programs. (2000). *A guide to the individualized education program.* U.S. Department of Education. https://www2.ed.gov/parents/needs/speced/iepguide/index.html

Rehabilitation Act of 1973, Section 504 Regulations, 34 C.F.R § 104.1.

US Office of Education (1977). Assistance to states for education of handicapped children: Procedures for evaluating specific learning disabilities. *Federal Register, 42*(250), 65082–65085.

Yell, M. L. (2019). *The law and special education* (5th ed.). Pearson Education.

6

Trauma-Informed Education

Contributed by Christy Berger

Over the years, scholars have researched the impacts of trauma on children and how it affects their learning and development. As a result, many educators and administrators are now working toward an educational approach called trauma-informed education. To lay the foundation for this chapter, we first need to define trauma. The Substance Abuse and Mental Health Services Administration's (SAMHSA, 2014) definition of trauma is, "Individual trauma results from an *event*, series of events, or set of circumstances that is *experienced* by an individual as physically or emotionally harmful or life-threatening and that has lasting adverse *effects* on the individual's functioning and mental, physical, social, emotional, or spiritual well-being." In other words, there must be an event that an individual experiences, which has lasting adverse effects. A key factor of this definition is that two people may experience the same event; however, their lasting effects may look different. By definition, trauma is truly a personal experience. According to research, there are three types of traumas (SAMHSA, 2014): *acute trauma* results from a single stressful or dangerous event; *chronic trauma* results from repeated and prolonged exposure to highly stressful events, and *complex trauma* results from exposure to multiple traumatic events.

Child welfare workers interact daily with children and families who have experienced trauma; therefore, it is essential to understand how best to support and work with each child by using evidence-based practices. In this chapter, we will use a fictional vignette to explore trauma, determine the appropriate supports for children, and answer the following questions:

1. What are adverse childhood experiences?
2. How does trauma manifest in children?
3. What is trauma-informed education?
4. How can I advocate for trauma-informed education?
5. Where can I find more information on trauma-informed education?

The office was quiet, the hum of the fluorescent lights the only sound. Sarah, a CASA volunteer, sat at her desk, flipping through a file. Her hands had become familiar with the folders and paperwork—sometimes it felt like that was all she ever did. But today was different. Today, she was preparing to meet with a family who had a story she wasn't sure she could fully understand. The family included a single mother and two middle school-aged girls, Elena and Elizabeth. From the paperwork, it showed that the girls had witnessed domestic violence, moved many times, and were in and out of trouble at school. Elena, the oldest daughter, stood out to Sarah because, per her file, she has had a variety of struggles in her short 13 years. Sarah noticed that Elena had difficulty connecting with adults at school and at home, and was unable to name any close friends. The notes also shared that last year, Elena had become very withdrawn at school, and her grades and attendance were in decline. In addition, she had two discipline reports for talking back and cursing at teachers. Her homeroom teacher reported that Elena was sleeping in class and that her appearance had also deteriorated. Sarah knew that she would have to work hard to build trust and connection with Elena, and to do so, she wanted to learn the effects of trauma and how schools could support children who have had such experiences.

What Are Adverse Childhood Experiences?

The Adverse Childhood Experiences (ACE) Study was a groundbreaking research project that explored the connection between childhood trauma and long-term health and well-being outcomes (See Center for Health Care Strategies, n.d.). It was conducted in the late 1990s by Dr. Vincent Felitti and Dr. Robert Anda, in collaboration with the Centers for Disease

Control and Prevention (CDC) and the Kaiser Permanente health system. The study showed that if individuals experienced traumatic events in their lives, such as abuse, neglect, or household dysfunction, the likelihood that they would have poor health outcomes and struggle in school was higher than for those who did not experience these events (ACE Interface, n.d.).

The study measured ten specific types of adverse childhood experiences (ACEs), grouped into three categories:

- Abuse: Physical, emotional, and sexual abuse.
- Neglect: Physical and emotional neglect.
- Household Dysfunction: Mental illness, substance abuse, domestic violence, parental separation/divorce, and having an incarcerated household member.

An ACE score is the compilation of "yes" responses to each of the ten survey questions; therefore, a person could have an ACE score from zero to ten. The most recent study from the CDC (2024) shows that nearly one in three students has an ACE score of 2 or 3.

Knowing a child's ACE score helps inform decisions on early interventions, improves mental health outcomes, promotes resilience, and ensures that resources are used effectively to mitigate the impact of childhood trauma. The goal is not to stigmatize children with high ACE scores but to empower caregivers, educators, and healthcare professionals to provide the right support and foster environments that help children thrive despite their challenges. According to Burke et al. (2011), 51 percent of children with an ACE score of four or higher had learning and behavioral problems in school, compared with only 3 percent of children with no ACE score. ACEs are the best predictor of poor health and the second-best predictor of academic failure.

How Does Trauma Manifest in Children?

One of the major ways that trauma manifests in children is through their stress response. There are three types of stress response: positive, tolerable, and toxic. Many of us experience positive stress responses, particularly

Table 6.1 Ten-Question Survey to Determine Adverse Childhood Experiences

Did a parent or other adult in the household often or very often . . . Swear at you, insult you, put you down, or humiliate you? *Or* Act in a way that made you afraid that you might be physically hurt?	Yes or No
Did a parent or other adult in the household often or very often . . . Push, grab, slap, or throw something at you? ***Or*** Ever hit you so hard that you had marks or were injured?	Yes or No
Did an adult or person at least 5 years older than you ever . . . Touch or fondle you or have you touch their body in a sexual way? ***Or*** Attempt or actually have oral, anal, or vaginal intercourse with you?	Yes or No
Did you often or very often feel that . . . No one in your family loved you or thought you were important or special? ***Or*** Your family didn't look out for each other, feel close to each other, or support each other?	Yes or No
Did you often or very often feel that . . . You didn't have enough to eat, had to wear dirty clothes, and had no one to protect you? ***Or*** Your parents were too drunk or high to take care of you or take you to the doctor if you needed it?	Yes or No
Were your parents ever separated or divorced?	Yes or No
Was your mother or stepmother . . . Often or very often pushed, grabbed, slapped, or had something thrown at her? ***Or*** Sometimes, often, or very often kicked, bitten, hit with a fist, or hit with something hard? ***Or*** Ever repeatedly hit at least a few minutes or threatened with a gun or knife?	Yes or No
Did you live with anyone who was a problem drinker or alcoholic or who used street drugs?	Yes or No
Was a household member depressed or mentally ill, or did a household member attempt suicide?	Yes or No
Did a household member go to prison?	Yes or No

when facing a deadline at work. In these situations, our body and mind shift into stress mode to help us stay focused and complete the task on time. However, if a child has had numerous traumatic experiences, their

Table 6.2 Cumulative Adverse Childhood Experiences Among US High School Students Aged <18 Years

ACE Score	0	1	2 or 3	4+
Female	18.3%	23.8%	34.1%	23.9%
Male	29.3%	25%	32.5%	13.3%

brains could be in a constant toxic stress response, which is a prolonged activation of stress that lacks protective relationships to bring them back to a normal state of being. Stressed brains do not learn as well as brains that feel safe, can emotionally regulate, and feel a sense of connection.

ACEs can have a profound effect on a child's developing brain, leading to disruptions in neurological, psychological, and emotional development. Early trauma can result in difficulties in emotional regulation, impaired relationships, and challenges in coping with stress, leading to a higher likelihood of engaging in unhealthy behaviors later in life. Similar to Elena in the vignette, her experience has led her to be cautious around and distrustful of others, as she has been hurt repeatedly. She withdraws from her peers and acts out in school, which are common trauma responses. Each child is unique, and their experiences with trauma can vary significantly, leading to different ways they cope or react to their feelings.

There are certain common behaviors, however, that might appear when working with children who have experienced trauma. These behaviors can manifest in a range of ways, such as

- **Avoidance behavior:** Children may attempt to avoid certain situations, people, or things that remind them of the traumatic experience. This could include avoiding school, specific social situations, or conversations that feel too personal.
- **Aggression:** Some children may act out aggressively due to the emotional pain they have experienced. Aggression could involve physical outbursts, verbal hostility, or even destructive behavior. The behavior may happen out of the blue or on a regular basis, depending on the child.
- **Difficulty with attachment to others:** Children who have experienced trauma may struggle to form healthy, trusting relationships with adults and peers. They might push people away, appear distant, or have difficulty connecting with teachers or peers, fearing that others might hurt them, leave them, or not understand their feelings.
- **Self-destructive behaviors:** In some cases, children may engage in self-harm or risky behaviors as a way to cope with overwhelming emotions or as a form of control over their circumstances. Self-destructive behaviors could include things like cutting, substance abuse, or engaging in reckless actions. It is important to remember that self-destructive behavior is not the same as suicidal ideation.

- **Isolation:** Trauma can lead children to withdraw from their peers and social environments. They may feel misunderstood, disconnected, or emotionally drained, leading them to seek solitude rather than interact with others.
- **Fatigue:** Children who have experienced trauma often feel emotionally exhausted. The constant stress and anxiety may leave them feeling physically tired. This fatigue can affect their ability to concentrate, participate in activities, or engage in daily routines. It's important to watch for changes in sleep patterns.
- **Difficulty with authority figures:** Children who have experienced trauma may have challenges with authority figures, such as teachers, parents, police, or other caregivers. They might resist guidance, struggle with discipline, or feel threatened by anyone in a position of power due to past experiences where they may have been mistreated or neglected.

Recognizing these behaviors is crucial in understanding the needs of traumatized children. With the right support, understanding, and care, these children can begin to heal and develop healthier coping strategies over time.

What Is Trauma-Informed Education?

Schools may use the language, 'trauma-informed,' 'trauma-sensitive,' or 'trauma-responsive practices,' and while the language is different, the core principles of the practices are not. According to Bath (2008), the three pillars of trauma-informed education are safety, connection, and managing emotional impulses. Similar to Maslow's hierarchy of needs (see Figure 6.1), safety is key for children to succeed at school. When discussing safety, both physical safety and emotional safety are important. Emotional safety for children refers to an environment where they feel safe, loved, and cared for. Many children come to school unsure of when they will get their next meal, where they will be sleeping that evening, or even if they will see their parents when they go home. Insecurity at home can start the child's day off in a toxic stress response, so schools must provide a safe environment for their students. Emotional safety could look like establishing rules, routines, or rituals so that the children know what to expect throughout their day. Many teachers use visual schedules and review them at the beginning of each day to check for any changes. Predictability is critical, as it can truly calm a child's nervous system during a toxic stress response and prime their brain for learning.

The second pillar is connection. There are many ways educators provide this opportunity each day with their students. An easy way to implement connections is through the use of community circles, which provide an opportunity for PK-12 students to build connections with their peers and teachers. Community circles are a purposeful dialogue process and a strategy for building relationships. All participants gather in a circle, facing one another. The shape of the circle is important—it ensures that everyone can see each other and fosters accountability through direct, face-to-face interaction. Circles promote equality and help reduce feelings of division. A circle can be as simple as the teacher starting the day with a question, unrelated to school, that each student can answer. The time dedicated to building connections in the classroom is key! Community circles are a tier 1 approach to building connections, which means they are good for all students. However, when school staff identify a student who may struggle with building connections, it is essential to create opportunities for direct connection-building with that child. These opportunities could include a mentor-mentee program, conducting a student interest inventory, or even having lunch with that student. The extra effort to build connections with students who have experienced trauma is vital to their academic success.

The last pillar of trauma-informed education is being able to manage emotional impulses. Being able to manage impulses is a skill that needs to be practiced daily by children and adults. The best way to proactively teach these skills in school is by using a social-emotional learning (SEL) curriculum. The Collaborative for Academic, Social, and Emotional Learning (CASEL, 2025) defines SEL as "an integral part of education and human development. Social/emotional learning is the process through which all young people and adults acquire and apply the knowledge, skills, and attitudes to develop healthy identities, manage emotions and achieve personal and collective goals, feel and show empathy for others, establish and maintain supportive relationships, and make responsible and caring decisions." SEL can be implemented in various ways within the school

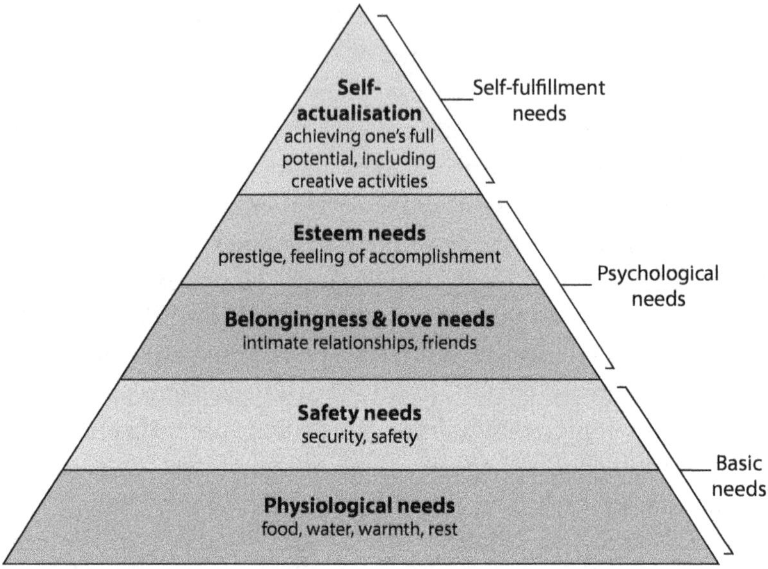

Figure 6.1. Maslow's hierarchy of needs. Note: Wikipedia contributors (2025).

building. It may look like a daily lesson provided by the teacher using an evidence-based SEL curriculum, or visuals of coping strategies to use when needed, or even proactively role-playing situations our students may face each day. SEL is designed to be proactive and taught with direct instruction to help students regulate their emotions.

Another approach to helping students learn how to manage their emotions is by establishing a "reset space." A reset space can be located within the classroom or in a separate area, designed to help students who may be struggling with their emotions, behavior, or concentration. It is a place where students can go when they need a break to calm down, refocus, or regain control before rejoining class activities. These spaces are typically set up with calming activities or sensory tools and are supervised by a staff member to ensure students feel supported. One essential component of a reset room is to proactively teach students how to use it while they are in a regulated state. The idea is to provide students with a safe and quiet environment where they can process their feelings, manage stress, and make positive decisions, helping them return to class in a better emotional state. Additional practices to teach students how to manage their emotional impulses could include small

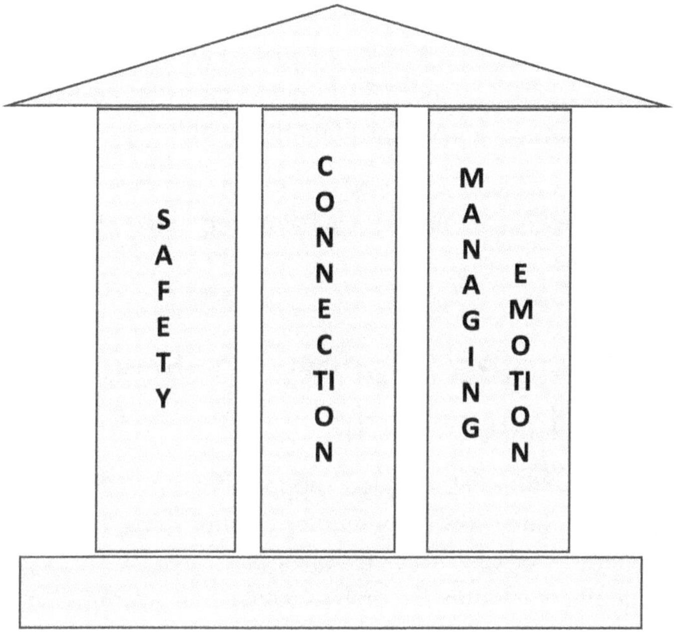

Figure 6.2. The three pillars of trauma-informed education. Note: Adapted from Bath (2008).

groups or one-on-one skill-building with the school counselor (see Figure 6.2).

Many schools organize their supports for students into three levels of intensity, often called "tiers." This tiered approach helps staff match the right level of support to each student's needs. Trauma-informed practices can be woven into each tier so that every student benefits, while students who have experienced significant trauma receive additional, targeted help.

Tier 1: Universal Supports for All Students

Tier 1 includes strategies and practices that every student in the school receives. These universal supports build a foundation of safety, predictability, and connection. Examples include:

- Clear, consistent classroom routines and school-wide expectations.
- Visual schedules and advance notice of changes to reduce anxiety.
- Regular community circles to build relationships and practice sharing feelings.

- School-wide social and emotional learning instruction that teaches skills like self-awareness, self-management, and problem-solving.
- Calm, respectful responses to behavior, with an emphasis on learning and repair rather than punishment.

For students who have experienced trauma, strong Tier 1 practices may reduce triggers, increase their sense of belonging, and prevent some crises before they occur.

Tier 2: Targeted Supports for Students Who Need More Help

Tier 2 includes additional, targeted supports for students who continue to struggle with behavior, emotions, or relationships, even when Tier 1 supports are in place. These strategies often involve small groups or increased adult connection. Examples include:

- Check-in/check-out with a trusted adult at the beginning and end of the school day.
- Small group skill-building focused on coping skills, emotional regulation, or social skills.
- Scheduled breaks or access to a reset space when the student begins to feel overwhelmed.
- Increased communication between school staff, caregivers, and child welfare workers to monitor patterns and adjust supports.

These targeted strategies can be especially helpful for children in foster care or under child protective services who may need more frequent reassurance, coaching, and structured opportunities to regulate their emotions.

Tier 3: Intensive, Individualized Supports

Tier 3 is designed for students with the most significant needs, whose trauma responses interfere with their ability to participate safely and successfully in school. Supports at this level are highly individualized and coordinated across systems. Examples include:

- Individual behavior support plans that are trauma-informed and focus on teaching replacement skills.
- Intensive counseling or therapy integrated with school supports, often involving a community mental health provider.
- Wraparound planning that brings together school staff, caregivers, child welfare workers, and other service providers to create a unified plan.
- Crisis plans that outline specific steps adults will take if the student becomes highly dysregulated, with an emphasis on safety and de-escalation.

By understanding the tiered supports available to students to assist in regulating their trauma responses, child welfare workers can better advocate for children in care.

How Can I Advocate for Trauma-Informed Education?

Child welfare workers play a crucial role in supporting children under child protective services, ensuring their needs are met, especially in school settings or during Individualized Education Program (IEP) meetings. Understanding trauma-informed education is the first step in advocating for this approach for the children you work with. By having the background knowledge on what trauma-informed education could look like, you can work to ensure that schools and educational settings understand and respond appropriately to the needs of students who have experienced trauma.

A second way to advocate is by encouraging collaboration with families/caregivers child welfare workers, and school personnel to ensure student success. This advocacy could be as simple as sharing relevant information about the child's history and any emotional or behavioral challenges they may face, keeping confidentiality requirements in mind, of course. Information sharing helps educators understand the context of a child's behavior and learning needs. In addition, this opens communication channels so that child welfare workers can track the child's academic progress and any behavioral issues in school, ensuring that interventions are working and advocating for adjustments when necessary.

By advocating for trauma-informed education, child welfare workers can help create a school environment where children affected by trauma feel safe, supported, and empowered to learn, thrive, and grow. Trauma-informed education not only benefits individual students but will also foster an environmental shift in how schools address and respond to the emotional and psychological needs of all students. The wonderful thing about trauma-informed education is that the practices can be adapted and implemented by a child welfare worker and family members in any setting. This holistic approach is beneficial for all students who have experienced trauma.

Where Can I Find More Information on Trauma-Informed Education?

- **Website:** *Revelations in Education*

  Revelations in Education offers numerous resources for parents, educators, and anyone working with children, including those related to neuroscience and trauma-informed practices. https://revelationsineducation.com/

- **Website:** *The National Child Traumatic Stress Network*

  This website provides a variety of information and resources around childhood trauma and stress. Specifically, there is a webpage dedicated to trauma-informed care. https://www.nctsn.org/trauma-informed-care

- **Book:** *The Trauma-Informed School: Administrator's Guide* by Jim Sporleder

  An all-inclusive guide designed to give school administrators of any school (elementary, middle, or high school) step-by-step instructions on how to turn a school of any size into a trauma-informed school. A great resource to show you what a trauma-informed school should look like and how to advocate for your child.

- **Book:** *Help for Billy*

This book by Heather Forbes is for parents and teachers addressing essential methods for managing the classroom behavior of a child with complex trauma.

- **Videos:** *Community Circle Examples*

  Each video provides an example of what a community circle can look like for younger students and older students.https://www.edutopia.org/video/60-second-strategy-community-circles (younger student). https://www.youtube.com/watch?v=qIel4r3uK9k (older students)

References

ACE Interface. (n.d.). *Home*. ACE Interface. https://www.aceinterface.com/

Bath, H. (2008). The three pillars of trauma-informed care. *Reclaiming Children and Youth, 17*(3), 17–21.

Burke, N. J., Hellman, J. L., Scott, B. G., Weems, C. F., & Carrion, V. G. (2011). The impact of adverse childhood experiences on an urban pediatric population. *Child Abuse & Neglect, 35*(6), 408–413. https://doi.org/10.1016/j.chiabu.2011.02.006

CASEL. (2025). *Collaborative for Academic, Social, and Emotional Learning.* www.casel.org

Centers for Disease Control and Prevention. (2024, March 10). *New CDC study highlights how preventing ACEs can reduce teen suicide attempts, prescription pain medication misuse, and more.* Morbidity and Mortality Weekly Report, 73 (Suppl. 4). https://www.cdc.gov/mmwr/volumes/73/su/su7304a5.htm?s_cid=su7304a5_w

Center for Health Care Strategies. (n.d.). *Original ACE questionnaire.* Center for Health Care Strategies. Retrieved March 10, 2025. https://www.traumainformedcare.chcs.org/resource/original-ace-questionnaire/

Substance Abuse and Mental Health Services Administration. (2014). *The relationship between adverse childhood experiences and alcohol use* (SMA 14-4884). Substance Abuse and Mental Health Services Administration. https://library.samhsa.gov/sites/default/files/sma14-4884.pdf

7

Supporting Students with High-Intensity Needs and Autism Spectrum Disorder

Many students with disabilities require significant support services to succeed in school and life. Among these, a subset of students exhibit what are termed "high-intensity needs." These needs manifest as significant and complex challenges across various domains, including academic, behavioral, emotional, social, and physical. These needs often require intensive, individualized interventions. While the term "high-intensity needs" lacks a precise, universally agreed-upon definition, it generally refers to students whose needs exceed the capacity of typical classroom settings and support systems (Cramer et al., 2023). The intensity is characterized by the severity, frequency, and pervasiveness of the needs, often resulting in significant disruption to their education and well-being. For these students, including the child in our next fictional vignette, a multi-tiered, intensive support system is essential to promoting success. This chapter centers on students with high-intensity needs, including those with Autism Spectrum Disorder (ASD). We will offer guidance to child welfare workers in identifying, supporting, and advocating for these students and seek to answer the following questions:

1. What are high-intensity needs, and how do they manifest?
2. What are the characteristics of Autism Spectrum Disorder?
3. What is the continuum of care, and where might students with high-intensity needs receive services?
4. How do I advocate for students with high-intensity needs?

5. Where can I learn more about advocating for students with high-intensity needs?

Jacob is a 10-year-old boy with high-intensity needs. More specifically, Jacob has intensive autism and resides in a residential treatment facility two hours from his assigned CASA, Mr. Lee. He has significant communication and behavioral challenges, requiring a structured environment with consistent support. Jacob's parents were unable to care for him and voluntarily terminated their parental rights when he was five. Since then, Jacob has spent time in various foster placements. For the past year, Jacob's needs were such that he required round-the-clock care at a residential treatment facility. At his current placement, Jacob uses a communication board to express his needs and receives Applied Behavior Analysis (ABA) therapy to help with behavior regulation and skill development. His days are structured with individualized interventions, sensory breaks, and social skills training, all of which are carefully monitored by his team. Despite this support, Jacob often struggles with transitions, which can lead to heightened anxiety and frustration. Mr. Lee understands the importance of his advocacy and makes the long drive each month to visit Jacob, ensuring that he remains informed about his well-being and progress. Mr. Lee has never worked with a child with high-intensity needs. Still, he takes detailed notes during each visit, documenting changes in Jacob's behavior, interactions, and overall demeanor. He later uses these notes to advocate for improvements in Jacob's care plan.

What Are High-Intensity Needs?

High-intensity needs, sometimes referred to as intensive support needs, in students represent a constellation of significant and multifaceted challenges that impact their ability to learn and fully participate in school. While lacking a universally agreed-upon definition, these needs exceed the capacity of typical classroom settings and standard support systems (National Association of State Directors of Special Education [NASDSE], n.d.). The defining characteristic is the combination of severity, frequency, and pervasiveness of challenges across multiple domains. These challenges often disrupt the student's education and overall well-being, usually requiring intensive, individualized interventions and a multi-tiered system of support for optimal outcomes. In a visual representation of multi-tiered systems of support (MTSS), students with high-intensity needs are often at the very top of the pyramid in the tier 1 category of interventions. Often, these students will be working toward alternative learning standards and may need support in areas such as academics, behavior, emotions, social skills, sensory needs, and physical needs (see Figure 7.1).

Academic Difficulties

Students may display profound and persistent learning challenges that defy typical interventions. These challenges might include intellectual disabilities resulting in significant skill deficits despite intensive support. These students may struggle with academic concepts that are far below

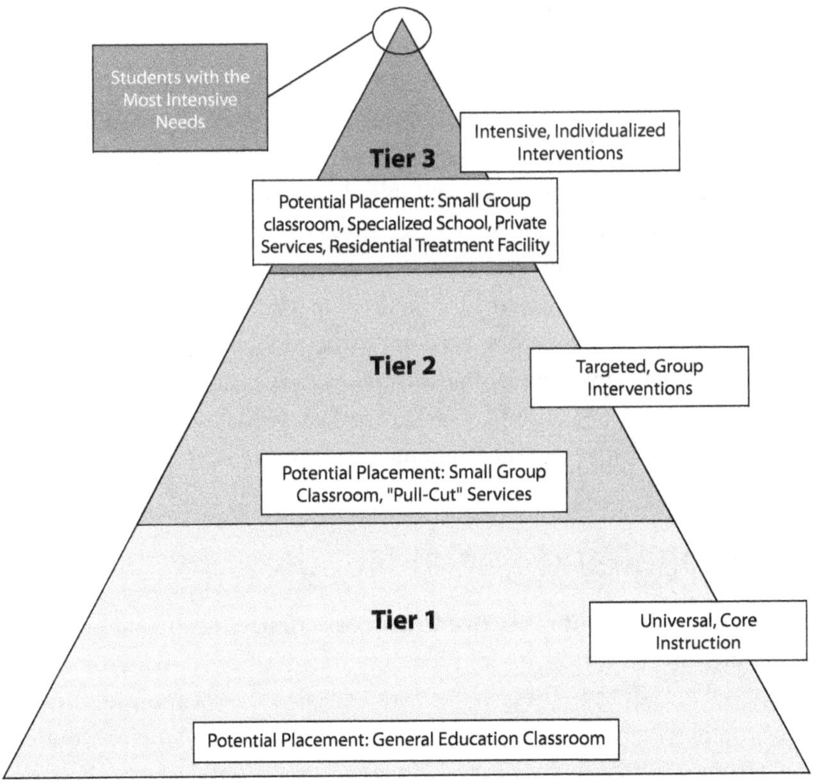

Figure 7.1. Multi-tiered systems of support and high-intensity needs.

what is typical for their age and grade level, requiring highly individualized instruction and adaptive learning materials. Intellectual assessments performed by a psychologist or educational diagnostician will identify the exact type of intellectual deficits (e.g., processing speed, perceptual reasoning, working memory) and their severity, comparing them to the general population. Significant gaps in foundational skills can also create cascading challenges across the curriculum, making it difficult to achieve academic progress on grade-level standards. These students often require specialized instructional approaches, assistive technologies, significant modifications to curriculum and assessment, and more individualized support. All of these components are important and should be addressed in the student's individualized education program (IEP).

Behavioral Challenges

Students with high-intensity needs may have severe and persistent behavioral issues, which may significantly disrupt the learning environment for the student and their peers (Lory et al., 2020). Noncompliance with classroom rules, frequent tantrums, and disruptive behavior are common concerns. However, aggression toward others or self-injury may be less common but more problematic behaviors exhibited by students with high-intensity needs. The frequency and intensity of these behaviors often necessitate a specialized Behavior Intervention Plan (BIP) and may require intensive behavioral interventions led by qualified specialists. Understanding the function of these behaviors through functional behavior assessments (FBAs) is crucial for developing effective interventions that address the underlying needs. As a child welfare worker, you should plan to attend these meetings for students with behavioral concerns.

Emotional and Social Needs

Students with high-intensity needs may experience significant emotional dysregulation, resulting in frequent meltdowns, shutdowns, or intense emotional instability. These behaviors can also be compounded by the abuse or neglect they experienced, as explained in Chapter 6. Students may struggle with anxiety, depression, and other mental health challenges that significantly impair their ability to focus, learn, and interact with peers (Qu et al., 2024). Profound social communication deficits may also be common, causing difficulties in understanding social cues, engaging in reciprocal interactions, and forming relationships. These deficits necessitate interventions, including social skills training, peer mentoring programs, and strategies for building positive relationships.

Physical Needs

The complexity of needs often extends to the physical realm. Students may have medical conditions (e.g., epilepsy, diabetes, ADHD) that require ongoing medical management and accommodations in the school setting (CEEDAR Center, 2024). Physical disabilities or mobility impairments may also necessitate adaptations to the learning environment. Additionally, students may require assistive devices or modifications to physical access within the building.

Sensory Sensitivities

Intense sensory sensitivities, common in conditions such as Autism Spectrum Disorder, can significantly affect a student's ability to function in school (Lynch & Irvine, 2009). These sensitivities might involve over- or under-responsiveness to light, sound, touch, taste, or smell, leading to anxiety, distress, and disruptive behaviors. Specialized strategies are needed to modify the learning environment, making it more comfortable and less overwhelming. These strategies include using noise-canceling headphones, providing a quiet space for breaks, adjusting seating arrangements, or modifying visual and tactile elements to create a more comfortable learning environment.

What Are the Characteristics of Autism Spectrum Disorder?

Autism Spectrum Disorder (ASD) is a complex neurodevelopmental condition affecting social communication, social interaction, and behavior. It is characterized by persistent difficulties across these areas, manifesting in a wide range of impacts and varying degrees of severity. The last point is key. As it is a "spectrum disorder," ASD varies greatly in its presentation and impact on growth in academic and functional skills. A phrase commonly attributed to Dr. Stephen Shore goes: "When you meet one person with autism, you've met one person with autism." Even so, the Diagnostic and Statistical Manual of Mental Disorders, 5th edition (DSM-5; American Psychiatric Association, 2013) describes two core domains of symptoms: deficits in social communication and restrictive, repetitive patterns of behavior.

Persistent Deficits in Social Communication and Social Interaction

This domain encompasses challenges across several areas, impacting a person's ability to connect with and understand others. These deficits may include challenges with social-emotional reciprocity, nonverbal communication, and building relationships (Harvard Health, n.d.).

- **Social-Emotional Reciprocity:** Difficulty engaging in back-and-forth interactions, sharing emotions or interests with others, and understanding nonverbal cues like facial expressions and body language. These deficits can lead to misunderstandings and make it difficult to build relationships.
- **Nonverbal Communication:** Problems with using or understanding nonverbal communication, including body language, eye contact, facial expressions, gestures, and tone of voice. Difficulties may range from subtle misinterpretations to a complete inability to utilize or decode these cues.
- **Developing, Maintaining, and Understanding Relationships:** Challenges in developing, maintaining, and understanding relationships appropriate to the developmental level. These deficits can include difficulty adjusting behavior to suit different social contexts, understanding social nuances, and experiencing challenges with friendships or peer interactions. There may be difficulties distinguishing between different types of relationships, such as friendships, romantic relationships, and family relationships.

Restricted, Repetitive Patterns of Behavior, Interests, or Activities

This domain reflects the tendency toward rigid and repetitive behaviors, interests, or activities. These patterns can include repetitive motor movements, inflexibility, fixated interests, and hyper- or hypo-reactivity to sensory sensitivities (American Psychiatric Association, 2013).

- **Stereotyped or Repetitive Motor Movements:** Repetitive movements or behaviors such as hand flapping, rocking, finger flicking, or lining up objects. These actions may serve as self-soothing or regulatory functions.
- **Insistence on Sameness, Inflexible Adherence to Routines:** An intense need for routines, predictability, and sameness in daily life. Changes to established routines can trigger significant distress or anxiety. Inflexible adherence to specific, nonfunctional routines can be disruptive to daily functioning.
- **Highly Restricted, Fixated Interests:** Developing intense, focused interests that are often unusual in their intensity or focus. These interests can consume a significant amount of time and energy, sometimes to the exclusion of other activities. These interests might include specific topics, objects, or activities that are pursued with exceptional intensity and focus.
- **Hyper or Hypo-reactivity to Sensory Input or Unusual Interest in Sensory Aspects of the Environment:** Unusual or heightened sensitivity to sensory input (e.g., sounds, lights, textures). This sensitivity can range from discomfort and avoidance to heightened fascination with specific sensory experiences. Sensory sensitivities can be significantly disruptive to daily functioning and may influence behaviors and preferences.

Variability in Severity

Again, ASD manifests on a spectrum, meaning symptoms vary significantly in type and intensity between individuals. Some individuals may require extensive support across all aspects of daily living, while others may need less-intensive assistance. There are also differences in the presence and severity of symptoms across the various domains, highlighting the individuality of presentations. For example, students may have difficulty engaging in back-and-forth conversations and recognizing social cues, but they may not exhibit repetitive motor movements or hyperreactivity to sensory input. Assessment of ASD, therefore, must account for the full range of potential symptoms to offer an appropriate diagnosis and a support plan that meets the specific individual's needs. Regardless of severity, students with ASD and other disabilities will receive their support on the continuum of care.

During one of Mr. Lee's visits, Jacob's behavioral therapist expresses concerns about his frequent self-injurious behaviors, which have increased despite current interventions. The staff are doing their best. However, they acknowledge that additional resources, such as a full-time one-on-one behavior technician and an expanded communication system, could significantly benefit Jacob. However, funding limitations have made fulfilling these requests difficult. Understanding the urgency of the situation, Mr. Lee works closely with Jacob's team to gather data, review his Behavior Intervention Plan (BIP) and Individualized Education Program (IEP), and consult with his ABA provider to determine additional effective strategies. He speaks with Jacob's caregivers, therapists, and teachers to get a comprehensive picture of his progress and struggles. Equipped with this thorough understanding, Mr. Lee schedules a meeting with facility administrators, his social worker, and special education representatives to advocate for Jacob's needs, knowing that a well-documented and evidence-based argument is the best way to secure the necessary support.

What Is the Continuum of Care, and Where Might Students with High-Intensity Needs Receive Services?

The continuum of care represents a range of educational placements and support services designed to provide the most appropriate level of intervention based on each student's individual needs (IRIS Center, n, d.).

This continuum begins with the least restrictive environment, the general education classroom, and extends to highly specialized settings, such as residential treatment facilities. The goal is always to place the student in the most inclusive and supportive setting possible while ensuring they receive the intensive services required to succeed. The continuum, as demonstrated in Figure 7.2, typically includes the following:

- **General Education Classroom with Supports:** The student remains in the general education classroom, receiving supplemental support services, such as tutoring, behavior support, or assistive technology.
- **Resource Room:** The student spends part of the day in a resource room with a special education teacher, receiving targeted academic and behavioral support.
- **Self-Contained Classroom:** The student is placed in a separate classroom with a special education teacher for all or most of the day, receiving intensive instruction and support.

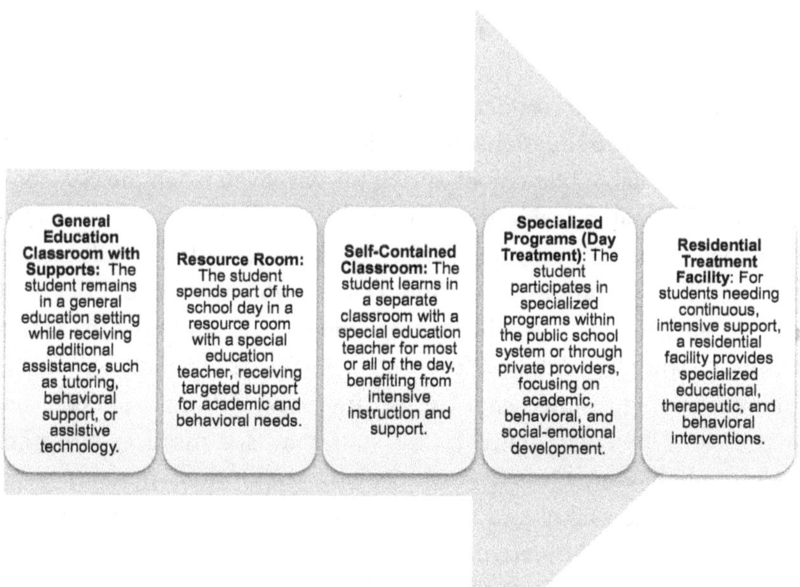

Figure 7.2. The continuum of services for students receiving special education services.

- **Specialized Programs (Day Treatment):** The student may receive services in specialized programs, either within the public school system or through private providers. These programs typically focus on intensive academic, behavioral, and social-emotional interventions.
- **Residential Treatment Facility:** A residential treatment facility may be necessary for students requiring intensive, around-the-clock support. These facilities provide specialized educational, therapeutic, and behavioral interventions, often for students exhibiting severe behavioral or emotional disturbances.

The location where a student receives services may vary based on several factors, including the level of support needed to meet the student's needs.

When a student with high-intensity needs lives in a residential treatment facility, there are always at least two systems involved in their daily life. One system is focused on treatment, safety, and daily living. The other is focused on providing a free appropriate public education through special education services. If these systems do not communicate clearly and consistently, important information can be lost and the student's progress can stall.

In many cases, the residential facility has its own on-site school or classroom. In other situations, the student lives in the residential facility but attends a local public school during the day. Even when the classroom is physically located inside the facility, there is still a school district or public agency that is responsible for the student's IEP and educational services. Child welfare workers should clarify which school district holds responsibility for the IEP, who the case manager is, and how the facility and school will share information.

Residential staff and school staff often have different perspectives on the same behavior. Direct care staff may see more evening and overnight behavior, while teachers see how the student manages group work, academic tasks, and transitions in a classroom. When these perspectives are combined, the team can create stronger behavior plans and supports. When they are not combined, each setting may create its own plan, which can be confusing or even contradictory for the student.

Effective collaboration between residential and school teams usually includes regular, planned communication rather than occasional crisis calls. This might look like scheduled check-ins between the facility case manager and the school case manager, joint meetings to update the IEP and behavior intervention plan, and shared data on behavior, communication, and skill development. When possible, the same de-escalation strategies, communication tools, and reinforcement systems should be used across settings so the student experiences predictability.

As a child welfare worker, you can support collaboration between residential and school teams by asking clear, practical questions such as

- Who is the primary school contact for this student, and who is the primary contact at the residential facility?
- How do the residential treatment plan and the IEP or 504 Plan fit together? Are they using the same goals and behavior strategies when possible?
- How often do the residential staff and school staff meet or communicate about this student? Is there a regular schedule for these conversations?
- Are residential staff invited to IEP meetings and given enough notice and information to participate meaningfully? Are school staff invited to treatment team meetings at the facility when educational issues are discussed?
- How are data about behavior, communication, and academic progress shared between the facility and the school? Who is responsible for collecting and sending this information?
- What is the plan for school when the student moves to a less restrictive placement, returns to a foster home, or changes facilities? Who will make sure the new school receives records and understands the student's needs on the first day?

For students like Jacob, strong collaboration between the residential facility and the school can reduce repeated assessments, prevent inconsistent expectations, and create a coordinated plan that supports both learning and treatment. Your role includes noticing when systems are working in isolation, naming that concern, and encouraging the adults at the table to plan together rather than separately.

How Do I Advocate for Students with High-Intensity Needs?

Regardless of the location of services, child welfare workers play a critical role in advocating for students with high-intensity needs. Advocacy for these students is like advocacy for all students with disabilities in the child welfare system, as explained in other chapters. As a reminder, effective advocacy involves understanding students' individual needs, collaborating with members of the IEP team, ensuring stability in the students' Least Restrictive Environment (LRE), and monitoring their progress.

Understanding Individual Needs

Effectively advocating for students with high-intensity needs begins with a thorough understanding of their unique challenges. This process goes beyond simply identifying a diagnosis; it requires a thorough examination of the individual's strengths, weaknesses, and specific needs across all domains: academic, behavioral, emotional, social, and physical (SAMHSA's Nation Child Traumatic Stress Network, n.d.). While students with less-intensive needs may be working toward meeting grade-level standards, children with high-intensity needs often require a greater focus on foundational skills that may not be considered traditional academic skills, such as eating, mobility, communication, and toileting. Considering that children with high-intensity needs make up a significantly smaller number of children receiving special education services, their unique needs may be new to you. A comprehensive assessment can help you better understand these needs and articulate the child's needs more effectively to those involved, including supervisors, foster parents, and the court. A comprehensive assessment includes input from parents, teachers, therapists, and, when appropriate, the student themself. This assessment must also account for the considerable impact of trauma. Again, understanding the nature and extent of any trauma experienced is paramount because trauma can dramatically affect a child's behavior, emotional regulation, and learning abilities (Shonkoff et al., 2012).

Careful consideration of the student's cultural background, linguistic needs, and developmental history is also integral for creating a truly person-centered approach to support. Beyond a comprehensive assessment, another way to gain insight into how to best advocate for the child is to speak with members of the IEP team and those who implement the child's services.

Collaboration with IEP Teams and Service Providers

Child welfare workers serve as vital links between the child, their family, and the educational system. Active participation in Individualized Education Program (IEP) meetings is not only encouraged, but it is essential. The worker must advocate effectively for the child's needs, ensuring the IEP accurately reflects the child's unique challenges and strengths and incorporates the most appropriate services and supports. This advocacy necessitates strong communication and collaborative teamwork with educators, therapists, and other professionals involved in the child's education (CEEDAR Center, 2024). The child welfare worker is one member of the collaborative team who ensures that the IEP addresses the child's academic, behavioral, social-emotional, and physical needs comprehensively and in the child's least restrictive environment. Importantly, the child welfare worker does not need to be an expert on every facet of the child's disability characteristics, needs, and services. Rather, pairing your understanding of special education law and procedures with your knowledge of the child, including their background and what you have gathered from visits, as well as their comprehensive assessment, will allow you to be an informed participant in these meetings. Ideally, child welfare workers will work collaboratively with the rest of the team to ensure the necessary support and resources are available to meet the child's needs.

Securing Necessary Resources

Students with high-intensity needs often require intensive education, healthcare, and housing services and support that go beyond what is typically needed for other children. Funding for these needs can come from a variety of sources, and it is essential for child welfare workers to gain insights into which agencies or funding streams provide the necessary support. Depending on their position, child welfare workers play a critical role in securing these resources. You may be applying for services on behalf of children in care. Frequently, child welfare workers may have to advocate for additional funding to support specialized therapies (e.g., occupational therapy, speech therapy, behavioral therapy), behavioral interventions, and assistive technology. Navigating the often complex bureaucratic processes involved in securing these resources requires persistence, advocacy, and collaboration with various agencies and stakeholders. Information gathered from your visits, work with service providers, and IEP documentation may serve as important data. Child welfare workers must regularly demonstrate a clear understanding of the necessary services, articulate their importance, and effectively communicate the child's needs to funding agencies and decision-makers.

Ensuring Placement Stability

Frequent changes in educational and housing placement can significantly disrupt a student's learning and emotional well-being. Child welfare workers work actively to maintain a consistent and supportive educational setting for the child, minimizing disruptions whenever possible and supporting the child through transitions as needed. This process requires careful coordination with schools and other agencies involved in the child's care. The child welfare worker should advocate for the least restrictive environment (LRE) that meets the child's educational needs, weighing the benefits of inclusion against the necessity of specialized support. This process is easier said than done, particularly in the most restrictive settings where there may be only one or two facilities capable of meeting students' intensive needs (IRIS Center, n.d.). Even so, child welfare workers regularly act as liaisons between the school, the child welfare system, potential placements, and healthcare providers, ensuring effective communication and collaboration to prevent unnecessary transitions. This approach minimizes potential trauma and maximizes opportunities for success and progress toward goals.

Monitoring Progress

Effective advocacy requires ongoing monitoring of the students' progress toward their IEP and life goals. Effective monitoring necessitates regular communication with the IEP team and close collaboration with educators, therapists, and service providers. Child welfare workers play a critical role in collecting data, interpreting progress, and advocating for necessary modifications to the IEP to ensure that the student continues to make progress. Data-driven decision-making, utilizing objective measures of progress, informs these crucial adjustments, ensuring the IEP remains responsive to the child's evolving needs and the realities of their circumstances. Furthermore, they often need to explain this progress, or lack thereof, to their supervisors, foster parents, biological parents, and the court.

During one of Mr. Lee's visits, Jacob's behavioral therapist expresses concerns about his frequent self-injurious behaviors, which have increased despite current interventions. The staff is doing their best. However, they acknowledge that additional resources, such as a full-time one-on-one behavior technician and an expanded communication system, could significantly benefit Jacob. However, funding limitations have made fulfilling these requests difficult. Understanding the urgency of the situation, Mr. Lee works closely with Jacob's team to gather data, review his Behavior Intervention Plan (BIP) and Individualized Education Program (IEP), and consult with his ABA provider to determine additional effective strategies. He speaks with Jacob's caregivers, therapists, and teachers to get a comprehensive picture of his progress and struggles. Equipped with this thorough understanding, Mr. Lee schedules a meeting with facility administrators, his social worker, and special education representatives to advocate for Jacob's needs, knowing that a well-documented and evidence-based argument is the best way to secure the necessary support.

As a child welfare worker, your role is vital in facilitating the success of these students by advocating for support for their complex challenges, which span academic, behavioral, emotional, and social domains. By understanding and identifying these high-intensity needs, you can collaborate effectively with caregivers, educators, and service providers to implement individualized interventions tailored to each student's unique circumstances. Jacob's story underscores the importance of your advocacy in securing the necessary resources and support services he requires. As emphasized in other chapters, this chapter highlights that comprehensive care for students with high-intensity needs hinges on strong collaboration and proactive communication, fostering an environment where students can thrive. As we consider the impact of such comprehensive support, it is essential to reflect on the foundation laid during early childhood.

Where Can I Learn More About Supporting Students with High-Intensity Needs and Autism Spectrum Disorder?

- **Book:** *High-Leverage Practices for Intensive Interventions.*

  This book is a comprehensive guide that focuses on effective strategies and methodologies for educators working with students who require intensive support in educational settings. The book is structured around high-leverage practices—strategies that have been shown to be particularly effective in improving outcomes for students with significant needs. https://www.routledge.com/High-Leverage-Practices-for-Intensive-Interventions/McLeskey-Maheady-Billingsley-Brownell-Lewis-Alber-Morgan/p/book/9781032231068?srsltid=AfmBOoqss8RfZCHDJZQRg__e-hduwJWhoaWAcK9nWHyE6SbImfke6UP2

- **Organization:** *Autism Speaks*

  Autism Speaks is a leading autism advocacy organization offering comprehensive information, resources, and support for families and professionals who work with children and adults with ASD. https://www.autismspeaks.org/

- **Organization:** *The Autistic Self Advocacy Network (ASAN)*

  ASAN is a grassroots organization run by and for people on the autism spectrum. Offering unique perspectives and resources, ASAN provides tools to advocate for policies that support disability rights and the needs of the Autistic community. https://autisticadvocacy.org/

References

American Psychiatric Association. (2013). *Diagnostic and statistical manual of mental disorders* (5th ed.). American Psychiatric Publishing, Inc.

CEEDAR Center. (2024, March). High leverage practices for students with disabilities (updated). University of Florida. https://ceedar.education.ufl.edu/wp-content/uploads/2024/03/High-Leverage-Practices-for-Students-with-Disabilties-updated.pdf

Cramer, E. D., Pham, A. V., Gonzalez, L., Gallo, R. F., & Freire, A. P. F. (2023). Collaborative preparation in equity-based practices to support minoritized students with high-intensity needs. In *Handbook of research on interdisciplinary preparation for equitable special education* (pp. 1–22). IGI Global. https://doi.org/10.4018/978-1-6684-6438-0.ch019

Harvard Health. (n.d.). *The formal diagnostic criteria for autism*. Harvard Medical School. https://adult-autism.health.harvard.edu/resources/the-formal-diagnostic-criteria-for-autism/

IRIS Center. (n.d.). *Least restrictive environment (LRE).* Vanderbilt University. https://iris.peabody.vanderbilt.edu/information-brief/least-restrictive-environment-lre/

Lory, C., Mason, R. A., & Davis, J. L. (2020). A meta-analysis of challenging behavior interventions for students with developmental disabilities in inclusive school settings. *Journal of Autism Developmental Disorders 50*, 1221–1237. https://doi.org/10.1007/s10803-019-04329-x

Lynch, S. L., & Irvine, A. N. (2009). Inclusive education and best practice for children with autism spectrum disorder: An integrated approach. *International Journal of Inclusive Education*, *13*(8), 845–859. https://doi.org/10.1080/13603110802475518

National Association of State Directors of Special Education. (n.d.). *High-intensity needs*. https://www.nasdse.org/

Qu, G., Shu, L., Liu, H., Ma, S., Han, T., Zhang, H., Huang, C., Wang, J., Yang, L., & Sun, Y. (2024). Association between adverse childhood experiences and academic performance among children and adolescents: A global meta-analysis. *Trauma, Violence & Abuse*, *25*(4), 3332–3345. https://doi.org/10.1177/15248380241246758

SAMHSA's National Child Traumatic Stress Network. (n.d.). *Trauma-informed care*. https://www.samhsa.gov/mental-health/trauma-violence/trauma-informed-approaches-programs

Shonkoff, J. P., Garner, A. S., Committee on Psychosocial Aspects of Child and Family Health, Committee on Early Childhood,

Adoption, and Dependent Care, and Section on Developmental and Behavioral Pediatrics, Siegel, B. S., Dobbins, M. I., Earls, M. F., … & Wood, D. L. (2012). The lifelong effects of early childhood adversity and toxic stress. *Pediatrics, 129*(1), e232–e246. https://doi.org/10.1542/peds.2011-2661

8

Early Childhood Special Education

Contributed by Dr. Marla J. Lohmann

As you read in Chapter 5, students with disabilities are supported as outlined in the Individuals with Disabilities Education Act (IDEA, 2004). This federal law ensures that all children with disabilities receive the supports and services needed to access educational and community activities with their typically developing peers. For children between the ages of 3 and 21, these services are outlined in Part B of IDEA and primarily provided within the school setting. For children between birth and their third birthday, the supports are described in Part C of IDEA and implemented in natural settings within the child's daily routines and activities.

Early childhood is generally considered to span from birth through the age of eight (National Association for the Education of Young Children, 2020). For children receiving special education services in the school setting, it typically extends from birth through the start of kindergarten. Approximately 77,000 infants and toddlers (U.S. Government Accountability Office, 2023) and between four and seven percent of preschoolers (Friedman-Krauss & Barnett, 2023) are diagnosed with a disability that qualifies for services and supports under IDEA. The most commonly identified primary disability among young children is a developmental delay (Friedman-Krauss & Barnett, 2023), and almost half of young children receiving special education services have an identified speech or language impairment as either their primary or secondary disability (Morgan et al., 2016). In addition, boys are more likely than girls to have a diagnosed disability in early childhood (Gordon et al., 2020), and young Black children are disproportionately identified with disabilities as compared to their Caucasian peers (Rausch et al., 2019).

In the course of their careers, child welfare workers are likely to encounter several young children with disabilities. In fact, almost a quarter of children in the foster care system have a medical diagnosis or a disability that qualifies for special education services, and children with disabilities are likely to remain in the foster care system for longer periods of time than other children (Platt & Gephart, 2022). About a third of children in the foster care system are under the age of six (Kids Count Data Center, 2025). With this in mind, child welfare workers need to understand how to identify young children who may have a disability and ways in which to support young children with diagnosed disabilities. In this chapter, a fictional vignette is used to discuss the early childhood special education process, with a specific focus on early intervention services (EI), and answer the following questions:

1. How are young children with disabilities identified?
2. How does early childhood special education differ from school-aged special education, and what is the difference between IDEA Part C and Part B?
3. What happens when a child turns three and is no longer eligible for early intervention services?
4. What are the common supports in preschool special education?
5. Where can I find out more about early intervention services?

Mr. Phiri is currently a Court Appointed Special Advocate (CASA) and has been working with one specific family for the past year. There are five children in the family, ranging in age from two to fifteen. Mr. Phiri has noticed that the youngest child, Precious, moves from one location to another by crawling and only uses the words "no" and "mama" to communicate her needs and desires. Mr. Phiri is not an expert on child development, but he does know that children should be walking and talking by their second birthday. He consults the Centers for Disease Control (CDC) guidance on early childhood developmental milestones. He learns that children should be walking by eighteen months and saying two-word phrases before their second birthday. Mr. Phiri has spoken with Precious's foster parents, and they share his concerns about her development. Mr. Phiri wants to figure out how to help Precious achieve the expected early childhood developmental milestones. With Mr. Phiri's encouragement, the foster parents contact Precious's pediatrician to inquire about the steps for assessing and identifying a potential disability.

How Are Young Children with Disabilities Identified?

Decades of research have supported the fact that early intervention services have both short-term and long-term benefits for young children with disabilities. Early intervention services, offered to infants and toddlers, are especially effective because young children's brains and bodies are still in the early stages of development, making them more responsive to interventions and supports (Tollan et al., 2023). Developmental gains are observed in all domains, including cognitive, social, physical, and communication, when young children receive early intervention services (Landa, 2018). Nonverbal children, especially those with autism spectrum disorder, who receive early intervention services have a higher likelihood of acquiring oral communication skills than do nonverbal children who do not receive these services (Koegel et al., 2013). In addition, early intervention services support families of children with disabilities by improving caregivers' skills in meeting their children's needs (Bailey et al., 2005). The specific legal requirements for identifying an infant or toddler with a disability are outlined in IDEA and referred to as the Infants and Toddlers with Disabilities Program. The verbiage found in IDEA is included in Textbox 8.1.

Textbox 8.1 The IDEA Definition of an Infant or Toddler with a Disability

§ 300.25 Infant or toddler with a disability.

Infant or toddler with a disability—

(a) Means an individual under three years of age who needs early intervention services because the individual—

(1) Is experiencing developmental delays, as measured by appropriate diagnostic instruments and procedures in one or more of the areas of cognitive development, physical development, communication development, social or emotional development, and adaptive development; or

(2) Has a diagnosed physical or mental condition that has a high probability of resulting in developmental delay; and

(b) May also include, at a State's discretion—

(1) At-risk infants and toddlers; and

(2) Children with disabilities who are eligible for services under section 619 and who previously received services under Part C of the Act until such children enter, or are eligible under State law to enter, kindergarten or elementary school, as appropriate, provided that any programs under Part C of the Act serving such children shall include—

(i) An educational component that promotes school readiness and incorporates pre-literacy, language, and numeracy skills; and

(ii) A written notification to parents of their rights and responsibilities in determining whether their child will continue to receive services under Part C of the Act or participate in preschool programs under section 619.

The referral, assessment, and identification process for young children suspected of having a disability differs from the process used for school-age children. Each state designs and implements its own early intervention program, meaning that the exact process may differ slightly, depending on the state in which you reside. However, the basic referral, assessment, and identification process remains the same and is outlined in Textbox 8.2. It is important to note that, under IDEA, early intervention programs have 45 calendar days after the initial referral for evaluation is made in order to complete the first seven steps outlined in the textbox.

The initial referral for assessment can be made by any stakeholder, but is commonly made by parents or caregivers, pediatricians, or childcare providers (Zero to Three, 2024). Once the referral is made, the child and family are assigned a Service Coordinator, who is responsible for guiding the family through the process and coordinating all services if the assessment indicates that the child qualifies for early intervention services (Nichols et al., 2025). Depending on the state, this person may also be an early intervention service provider, such as the early childhood special educator or physical therapist, or they may be responsible for service coordination but not directly deliver services. The Service Coordinator is the primary point of contact for families and other stakeholders who have questions about the process. When child welfare workers have questions about early intervention, the assessment process, or the delivery of special education services, they should contact the Service Coordinator.

Textbox 8.2 The Early Intervention Referral, Assessment, and Identification Process

1. A referral for evaluation is made by a stakeholder involved with the child.
2. The child's family/caregivers are assigned a Service Coordinator, who will be their main point of contact to support them through the assessment and identification process and will continue supporting them if services are later provided.
3. The child's family/caregivers will provide written consent for an evaluation to occur. No portion of the evaluation may occur before that consent is provided.
4. An evaluation of developmental skills will be completed by a trained evaluation team, which may include medical providers, an early childhood special educator, a speech-language pathologist, an occupational therapist, a physical therapist, a nutritionist, a social worker, and any other qualified early childhood professional.
5. The evaluation team and the child's family/caregivers will meet to determine if the evaluation results indicate the child is eligible to receive early intervention services and in which developmental areas the child qualifies.
6. The early intervention team and child's family/caregivers will collaborate to identify the child's needs, as well as the needs

of the family, with a specific focus on family needs that directly impact the child's development.

7. The early intervention team and child's family/caregivers will hold a meeting to develop the Individualized Family Service Plan (IFSP), which outlines the services and supports that will be provided to both the child and the family.

The child's family/caregivers will provide consent for the supports and services outlined in the IFSP to be implemented. After that consent is provided, service delivery may begin. No services may be provided until consent is given.

Early intervention assessments are conducted by a team of professionals that might include an educator, related service providers, and community representatives. The exact team membership will be determined by the specific child's needs, as well as state and local policies and procedures. The assessment team will evaluate the child's needs in all areas of suspected disability and consider how the family's needs impact the child's development. Based on that evaluation, the team will make recommendations on whether the child qualifies for early intervention services and which specific services would best support them. The entire team, including the family and other stakeholders, will meet to discuss the recommendations and develop a plan to support the child. If possible, it is beneficial for child welfare workers to attend these meetings to provide input about the child and advocate for the services and supports that best meet the child's developmental needs.

After Precious's pediatrician confirms that Precious is not meeting developmental milestones, Mr. Phiri contacts the state early intervention agency and makes a referral for Precious to receive an evaluation. Mr. Phiri is hopeful that this step will ensure Precious will soon receive the services and supports to help her reach the developmental milestones of early childhood. Nevertheless, he is curious how the process will work. He has had previous experiences working with children who receive special education services in the K-12 school setting, but this is his first time advocating for a child who might receive early intervention services. He wonders what the process and the supports offered will be like.

How Does Early Intervention Differ from School-Aged Special Education?

Early intervention services differ from school-age services in several ways. First, early intervention is family centered, not child centered. This model of support is based on the belief that young children are best supported through a systems approach, which involves ensuring the family system is equipped to meet the unique developmental needs of the child with a disability (McCarthy & Guerin, 2022). The second difference is the location of the service delivery. While school-age services are provided in school settings, early intervention services are typically offered in natural settings and integrated into daily activities.

In most cases, early intervention providers travel to young children's homes, daycares, or other community-based locations in order to provide the services outlined in the IFSP. To the extent possible, these services are integrated into children's daily routines and embedded in play-based activities. Because supports are provided in childcare centers or other environments with typically developing children, children receiving early intervention services receive an early childhood education that is similar to, or identical to, that of their peers. Thirdly, while all services outlined in the Individualized Education Program (IEP) for children aged three to twenty-one are offered free of charge, some early intervention services may have a fee associated with them. Child Find services, assessments and evaluations, service coordination, and the development of the Individualized Family Service Plan (IFSP) are all provided at no cost. Depending on the specific way in which your state implements early intervention services, the services and supports outlined in the IFSP may be offered based on a sliding-scale fee or may be billed to the family's health insurance. Additionally, early intervention services are not provided by a single agency. Instead, the goal of early intervention is to coordinate existing services provided by various community agencies, ensuring that the child's and family's unique needs are met and that the child can make progress toward age-appropriate developmental milestones. This service coordination is conducted by the State Interagency Coordinating Council (SICC). Finally, early intervention is different from school-based special education services because the supports provided to the child are outlined in the IFSP, instead of the IEP. The IFSP team must meet every six months to update the document, while IEP teams are mandated to meet at least annually. Textbox 8.3 outlines the required components of the IFSP. Some early intervention programs may choose to include additional information, but the listed components are required under IDEA.

Textbox 8.3 The Required Components of the Individualized Family Service Plan (IFSP)

1. An explanation of the child's present developmental levels in all domains (physical, cognitive, communication, social/emotional, and adaptive)
2. Information about the child and family, including their identified needs
3. Expected outcomes of early intervention for both child and family, including a description of how those outcomes will be assessed
4. The specific services that will be provided to meet the identified needs of the child and family and information about those services including: (a) the anticipated start and end dates of services, (b) the frequency and length of each service session, (c) the location of service delivery, and (d) the method of service delivery (e.g., direct service, indirect service, consultation).
5. An explanation of funding, including what services will be provided at no charge, the services that will be billed to health insurance, and the services for which the family is financially responsible.
6. A plan for supporting the child in the transition from early intervention services to school-age services at the age of three
7. The name and contact information of the Service Coordinator
8. Signatures of all members of the IFSP team

After working closely with the early intervention providers and participating in the development of the IFSP, Mr. Phiri feels confident that Precious will have her needs met. After only a few months, he is already seeing progress in her development and has noticed that she is now walking instead of crawling and is speaking using short phrases to express her needs and desires. Mr. Phiri knows, though, that early intervention is only designed to support children until their third birthday and is concerned about what will happen to Precious in six months, once she is no longer eligible for early intervention services. He wants to better understand the process for transitioning children from early intervention services to school-based special education.

What Happens When a Child Turns 3 and Is No Longer Eligible for Early Intervention Services?

Early intervention services are designed to support children from birth to their third birthday. Once they reach the age of three, young children with disabilities are supported under Part B of IDEA and are supported in school-based settings. This means that preschoolers with disabilities may transition from early intervention to school-age services at any time during the year, typically on their birthday. At this time, the child is supported through the processes described in Chapter 5. During the preschool years, from a child's third birthday until they begin kindergarten, the services provided are covered under Section 619 of Part B of IDEA. According to the U.S. Department of Education (2024), about a third of preschoolers with disabilities attend an inclusive early childhood program alongside their typically developing peers and receive special education services integrated into that program. Another third attend an inclusive early childhood program but receive special education services in a separate location. A third of young children with disabilities receive special education services in a special education classroom or school, in their homes, or another setting outside of the school.

While children are receiving early intervention services, the IFSP team must develop a plan for transition activities to ensure the child's needs are met once they reach the age of three. The team must meet at least three months before the child's third birthday to develop a plan, but it is best practice to meet earlier than that and discuss the transition plan at every IFSP meeting. The transition planning process should include (a) discussions about the child's current expected outcomes as outlined in the IFSP and potential future IEP goals, (b) any assessments that must be completed before the child's third birthday and who will conduct those assessments, (c) timelines for completing required transition tasks, (d) the concerns or needs of any team members, (e) an explanation of how services will be determined and delivered in the school setting, and (f) the roles and responsibilities of each team member. As a child welfare worker, there are various topics and considerations you should be prepared to discuss or ask about at these meetings (Textbox 8.4).

Textbox 8.4 Discussion Topics and Questions for Early Intervention Transition Planning

1. Ensure that you understand the differences between early intervention and school-based special education services.
2. Concerns of the family/caregivers or yourself regarding the child's needs
3. Where will/can services be provided, and how are decisions made regarding service delivery location?
4. What options are available for transportation to/from the school or preschool program?
5. In what ways can families/caregivers be involved in the preschool classroom and the child's education?
6. To what extent will the child receive instruction and services/supports with their typically developing peers?
7. What specific supports will the early intervention program, especially the Service Coordinator, provide during the transition process?
8. Who will be the contact person(s) in the school when questions arise?

In the months leading up to this transition, the child and their families or caregivers will visit the school and the preschool classroom and meet the teachers who will be working with the child. For some children, one visit will be organized, while other schools have each child visit individually as frequently as necessary during the transition period. These visits are important because they are intended to ease the transition and help the child feel comfortable in the new setting. Child welfare workers should plan to attend these visits with the child or schedule their own visits to better understand the learning environment where the child will be going. When families, caregivers, and other advocates for the child believe the child needs additional visits and exposure to the preschool during the transition period, they should request this and advocate for including multiple visits as part of the transition process outlined in the IFSP. The child will likely have many questions about their new school and upcoming changes that might occur, so child welfare workers should be prepared to answer questions and support the child through the transition from early intervention services to early childhood special education.

Mr. Phiri attended Precious' transition meetings and asked each of the questions outlined above. In addition, he went with Precious and her foster family to visit the preschool classroom on three separate days. While there, he had conversations with the preschool teacher to ensure she understood what Precious needed to be successful. Mr. Phiri feels confident that Precious will have her needs met in the preschool classroom and will benefit from the opportunity to interact with typically developing peers on a regular basis.

What Are the Common Supports in Preschool Special Education?

Once young children with disabilities enter the public school system, the special education services they receive change and become school-based and focused on the needs of the child and not the family. Specific differences between early intervention and school-age services are outlined in Figure 8.1. Preschool special education services are offered

Early Intervention Services	Both Early Intervention and School-Age Services	School Age Services
• Family-Centered • Supports provided in natural settings • Focus is on supporting young children in meeting developmental milestones • Part C of IDEA • Support plan outlined in Individualized Family Service Plan (IFSP)	• Mandated under federal law • Support children with disabilities • Provide individualized supports • Include both educational supports and related services • Include transition planning activities	• Child-centered • Supports provided in school setting • Focus is on ensuring access to academics • Part B of IDEA • Specially designed instruction outlined in Individual Education Program (IEP)

Figure 8.1. Comparison of early intervention services and school-age special education services.

in a variety of formats, with wide differences between various states and school districts. In some cases, children with disabilities are educated in a general education early childhood classroom, such as a Head Start program or state-funded preschool program located in the public school setting. In these classrooms, all children are taught by a general education teacher who receives support from a special education team, which might include an early childhood special education teacher and classroom assistants. In other cases, young children with disabilities may be educated in early childhood special education classrooms that are taught by a special education teacher and include children with disabilities and some typically developing peers. This educational placement is more common for children with significant support needs. Finally, some young children with disabilities attend preschools in their communities and either travel to the public school setting to receive special education services as needed or have early childhood special educators and related service providers visit them to offer the necessary supports.

The increase in state-funded and universal preschool programs nationwide is also affecting the field of preschool special education, leading to a higher number of young children receiving special education services in community-based early childhood programs. An additional consideration that affects the location of services for many young children with disabilities is that some states and school districts do not offer full-day options for preschoolers with disabilities, requiring some families to opt out of special education services until the child reaches kindergarten (Steed et al., 2024). Child welfare workers can aid in the selection of the appropriate placement for the child by understanding the various placement options available in the community and advocating for the one that best meets the developmental needs of the child, as well as the logistical needs of the child's caregivers.

For young children, early childhood special education services are embedded in daily routines and activities, including structured group activities and unstructured playtimes (Sheppard & Moran, 2022). Early childhood teachers and related service providers incorporate learning activities that support progress toward IEP goals during these sessions (Odom, 2000). For example, the early childhood special education teacher may lead Circle Time for all children in the classroom and select learning materials, such as books, songs, and interactive activities, that benefit all children while targeting the needs of children with disabilities. Alternatively, the school speech-language pathologist may lead a small group of children in language-focused activities during Center Time. The physical and occupational therapists may join the children on the playground during outdoor play to ensure that children with disabilities have the support needed to access playtime with their peers.

Once the child enters the early childhood special education program, child welfare workers should continue to check on their progress and maintain regular communication with the child's IEP team. It is likely that the child will continue to have questions, concerns, and needs as they adjust to the school setting, so the role of the child welfare worker is vital at this stage.

During the transition planning process, the team determined that Precious needs would be best met in an inclusive state-funded preschool program. After a few months, Mr. Phiri notes that Precious is speaking more words and has learned to run and ride a tricycle, which helps her keep up with her peers. He is thrilled to see the progress that Precious has made and is glad that he took the time to better understand the early intervention and early childhood special education processes. He now feels empowered to support other young children who may need early childhood special education services.

Where Can I Find More Information About Early Childhood Special Education and Early Intervention Services?

This chapter offered a brief overview of early intervention services and early childhood special education services. If, and when, you get the opportunity to support a young child with a disability (or suspected disability), you will likely have additional questions. The following resources can help you learn more about meeting the needs of young children with disabilities.

- **Website**: *Centers for Disease Control and Prevention*

  The first link from this website offers an overview of early intervention services and includes links to the websites for each state's early intervention programs. These links provide guidance on the referral, assessment, and service delivery processes for the state, as well as contact information for state early intervention personnel. Additionally, the second link provides an overview of the expected developmental milestones for children from birth to age five. Child welfare workers can consult this information to gain a better understanding of the skills that young children should master by a certain age.

  https://www.cdc.gov/ncbddd/actearly/parents/states.html
  https://www.cdc.gov/ncbddd/actearly/milestones/index.html

- **Website**: *Center for Parent Information and Resources*

  This website provides information about various aspects of the early intervention process and includes a Parent's Record-Keeping Worksheet that can be used to track children's progress toward developmental milestones. This makes it a valuable tool for collecting data to share with early intervention providers during the referral process.

  https://www.parentcenterhub.org/ei-overview/

- **Website**: *OSEP Fast Facts: Children 3 Through 5 Served Under Part B, Section 619 of the IDEA*

  This fact sheet from the U.S. Department of Education provides statistics on preschoolers receiving special education services, including information on the number of children being served, demographic data about those children, service delivery locations, and the percentage of young children identified with each of the disability categories outlined in IDEA. https://sites.ed.gov/idea/osep-fast-facts-children-3-5-20

- **Website**: *Early Intervention Training Program at the University of Illinois*

  This website offers a variety of resources related to early intervention, with a specific focus on the Individualized Family Service Plan (IFSP). The website includes guidance on writing the IFSP, a sample IEP with a meeting agenda, and blank IFSP and agenda templates that teams can use as they meet to develop a child's IFSP. https://blogs.illinois.edu/view/6039/114604

- **Book**: *Handbook of Early Childhood Intervention (2nd edition)* edited by Shonkoff & Meisels.

  While this book is over twenty-five years old, it is considered a seminal work in early intervention. It is specifically written to support various service providers, including child welfare workers.

- **Video Library**: *The Early Childhood Personnel Center (ECPC)*

  This video library provides links to nearly 500 videos from various sources, offering specific information on topics related to early childhood intervention, including assessment, intervention, and instructional practices. https://ecpcta.org/video-library/

References

Bailey, D. B., Hebbeler, K., Spiker, D., Scarborough, A., Mallik, S., & Nelson, L. (2005). Thirty-six month outcomes for families of children who have disabilities and participated in early intervention. *Pediatrics, 116*(6), 1346–1352. https://doi.org/10.1542/peds.2004-1239

Friedman-Krauss, A. H., & Barnett, W. S. (2023). *The State(s) of Early Intervention and Early Childhood Special Education: Looking at Equity*. National Institute for Early Education Research.

Gordon, R. A., Sheridan, K., Bates, J., deSouza, S., & Pradzinski, A. (2020). Child care arrangements and gender: A national portrait of preschool-aged children. *Early Childhood Research Quarterly, 53*(4), 40–49. https://doi.org/10.1016/j.ecresq.2020.02.003

Individuals with Disabilities Education Act of 2004, 20 U.S.C. § 1400

Kids Count Data Center. (2025). Children in foster care by age group in United States. https://datacenter.aecf.org/

Koegel, L. K., Koegel, R. L., Ashbaugh, K., & Bradshaw, J. (2013). The importance of early identification and intervention for children with or at risk for autism spectrum disorders. *International Journal of Speech-Language Pathology, 16*(1), 50–56. https://doi.org/10.3109/17549507.2013.861511

Landa, R. J. (2018). Efficacy of early interventions for infants and young children with, and at risk for, autism spectrum disorders. *International Review of Psychiatry, 30*(1), 25–39. https://doi.org/10.1080/09540261.2018.1432574

McCarthy, E. & Guerin, S. (2022). Family-centred care in early intervention: A systematic review of the processes and outcomes of family-centred care and impacting factors. *Child: Care, Health, and Development, 48*(1), 1–32. https://doi.org/10.1111/cch.12901

Morgan, P. L., Hammer, C. S., Farkas, G., Hillemeier, M. M., Maczuga, S., Cook, M., & Morano, S. (2016). Who receives speech/language services by 5 years of age in the United States?. *American Journal of Speech-Language Pathology, 25*(2), 183–199. https://doi.org/10.1044/2015_AJSLP-14-0201

National Association for the Education of Young Children. (2020). *Developmentally appropriate practice: A position statement*. National Association for the Education of Young Children. https://www.naeyc.org/resources/position-statements/dap/contents

Nichols, S., Schnurr, M. P., Hill, C. F., Hardison, M. P., & Kastanis, M. P. (2025). Establishing knowledge and skills for service coordinators in early intervention. *Infants & Young Children*, 38(1), 40–55. https://doi/org/10.1097/IYC.0000000000000281

Odom, S. L. (2000). Preschool inclusion: What we know and where we go from here. *Topics in Early Childhood Special Education, 20*(1), 20–27.

Platt, C., & Gephart, S. M. (2022). Placement disruption of children with disabilities in foster care. *Journal of Pediatric Nursing, 66*, 30–35. https://doi.org/10.1016/j.pedn.2022.05.004

Rausch, A., Joseph, J., & Steed, E. (2019). Dis/ability critical race studies (DisCrit) for inclusion in early childhood education: Ethical considerations of implicit and explicit bias. *Zero to Three, 40*(1), 53–51.

Sheppard, M. E., & Moran, K. K. (2022). The role of early care providers in early intervention and early childhood special education systems. *Early Childhood Education Journal, 50*(6), 891–901. https://doi-org.ezproxy.ccu.edu/10.1007/s10643-021-01225-x

Steed, E. A., Strain, P. S., Rausch, A., Hodges, A., & Bold, E. (2024). Early childhood administrator perspectives about preschool inclusion: A qualitative interview study. *Early Childhood Education Journal, 52*(3), 527–536. https://doi-org.ezproxy.ccu.edu/10.1007/s10643-023-01448-0

Tollan, K., Jezrawi, R., Underwood, K., & Janus, M. (2023). A review on early intervention systems. *Current Developmental Disorders Reports, 10*(2), 147–153. https://doi.org/10.1007/s40474-023-00274-8

U.S. Department of Education. (2024). *OSEP fast facts: Children 3 through 5 served under Part B, Section 610 of IDEA.* https://sites.ed.gov/idea/osep-fast-facts-children-3-5-20

U.S. Government Accountability Office. (2023). *Special education: Additional data could help early intervention programs reach more eligible infants and toddlers.* https://www.gao.gov/assets/gao-24–106019.pdf

Zero to Three. (2024). *What you need to know: Early intervention.* https://www.zerotothree.org/resource/what-you-need-to-know-early-intervention/

9
Transition Planning

Whether between schools, placements, or stages in life, transitions can be stressful and upsetting times for youth, particularly for youth with disabilities in foster care. The transition from secondary school to adulthood, in particular, is a pivotal stage in life, filled with promise and potential. For many young people, it is a time of exploration, new beginnings, and exciting possibilities. However, for youth in foster care, especially those with disabilities, this transition can be significantly more challenging. They may encounter instability in their living situations, inconsistent access to vital support services, and a lack of ongoing family guidance that many take for granted. This chapter examines the unique difficulties faced by these vulnerable youth with disabilities as they prepare to navigate adult life. We will explore the crucial role of transition planning, a legally mandated aspect of the Individuals with Disabilities Education Act (IDEA), and how child welfare workers can best assist students with disabilities through this complex process. Using a fictional vignette, this chapter showcases best practices in transition planning, highlighting the principles of person-centered planning and self-determination as cornerstones of successful transitions. The following questions will be answered:

1. What is a transition plan, and what are its components?
2. What questions should I ask in a transition planning meeting?
3. How can I help youth transition effectively into a new placement, school, and post-secondary opportunities?
4. Where can I find more information about transition plans and post-secondary transition?

Sam, a new foster care social worker, recently received a new addition to her caseload: Jessica, a 16-year-old girl. Jessica was diagnosed with dyslexia and an emotional and behavioral disorder and has been in and out of foster care since age 10, experiencing multiple placement changes and frequent school disruptions. Despite these challenges, she possessed remarkable artistic talent and expressed a strong desire to attend art school after high school graduation. Her current foster parents enthusiastically support this goal. However, her history of instability looms large. Her academic record reflected the significant gaps caused by her frequent moves and inconsistent access to support services. Her current foster parents, while dedicated and supportive, lack experience navigating the complexities of special education transition planning and are understandably anxious about her future.

What Is a Transition Plan, and What Are Its Components?

Transition planning in special education, as mandated by the IDEA (2004), is a legally required component of the Individualized Education Program (IEP) for students with disabilities. It is typically initiated around age 14 and formalized by age 16. It serves as a blueprint for a successful transition from school to post-school activities, encompassing a comprehensive strategy to support the students' progress toward achieving their educational, independent living, and vocational goals. The term vocational education is commonly referred to as career and technical education. A foster care transition plan, in contrast, is a comprehensive roadmap designed to prepare a young person in foster care for independent living as they approach the age of emancipation (typically 18 but can vary by state). A foster care transition plan is an important document outlining the steps and support needed to help the youth successfully transition from the foster care system to self-sufficiency. Unlike a special education transition plan, which focuses primarily on educational and vocational goals, a foster care transition plan encompasses a much broader range of aspects necessary for independent living. As a child welfare worker, you may be familiar with the process of developing a foster care transition plan; however, a special education transition plan has several unique components, as mandated by IDEA.

Components of a Transition Plan

A special education transition plan is centered on collaboration between several important stakeholders. A team-based approach necessitates open communication and coordinated efforts among various stakeholders (Gershwin, 2022). These stakeholders include but are not limited to the student, whose voice and self-determination are central to the process (Wehmeyer, 2009), their parents or guardians, special and general education teachers, school counselors, related service providers (i.e., occupational therapists, physical therapists, speech-language pathologists, counselors, etc.), and vocational rehabilitation counselors, and, critically for students in foster care, child welfare (Figure 9.1).

Regular meetings, utilizing effective communication strategies as discussed in Chapter 4, are essential for maintaining open lines of communication and ensuring everyone remains informed and aligned. Effective communication may involve using various methods, including regular email updates, shared online platforms for documentation, formal

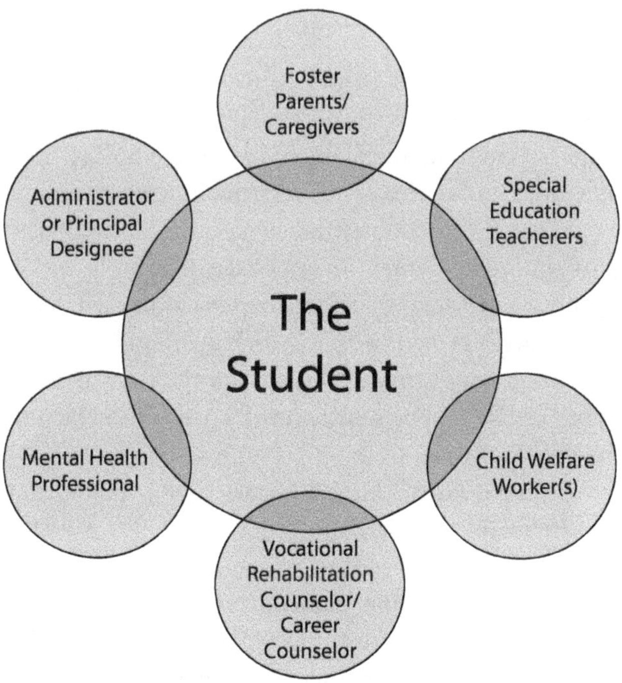

Figure 9.1. Potential participants in transition planning.

meeting minutes, and informal check-in meetings, to strengthen relationships and facilitate collaboration. This collaborative effort ensures a holistic understanding of the student's needs and aspirations.

Central to effective transition planning is a comprehensive assessment of the student's strengths, needs, and potential. This assessment goes beyond academic achievement to encompass job-related interests, social-emotional skills, and independent living abilities and opportunities. Multiple assessment tools and strategies are employed, including formal and informal assessments (IRIS Center, n.d.). Formal assessments include surveys, standardized tests, and vocational inventories. Informal assessments, in contrast, include information gathered from non-standardized assessments. Taken together, these tools generate a holistic understanding of students' capabilities and challenges. These assessments inform the development of personalized, measurable goals for post-school life, recognizing and respecting the student's cultural background and language proficiency to ensure culturally responsive planning (Rossetti et al., 2020). The student's active participation in the assessment and goal-setting phases is paramount as it fosters self-determination and ensures that the resulting plan aligns with their vision for the future and goals (Bateman, 2017).

The transition plan details specific, measurable, achievable, relevant, and time-bound (SMART) goals across the key domains of education/training, employment, and independent living (Hedin & DeSpain, 2018). These goals should be concrete, with actionable steps toward post-school success. Examples include obtaining a specific vocational certificate, securing part-time employment in a chosen field by a certain date, or establishing independent living arrangements within a defined timeframe. These clear objectives provide a framework for monitoring progress and facilitating necessary adjustments throughout the transition journey. The plan also specifies the supports and services needed to reach those goals; this may involve vocational training programs, job coaching, instruction in independent living skills, counseling, assistive technology, healthcare services, or housing support, all tailored to the student's unique circumstances.

Finally, successful transition planning requires ongoing monitoring and evaluation. Regular progress should be tracked by collecting and analyzing data to determine whether the student is meeting their goals. The information gathered is then used to make any necessary adjustments

Table 9.1 Postsecondary Goals and Activities

Educational Goals	
SMART Goal	**Activity**
Research and visit at least three colleges or training schools within the next six months.	Attend college fairs, take campus tours, and speak with admissions counselors.
Meet with at least two students or professionals who have pursued a career of interest within the next three months.	Join mentorship programs or attend networking events.
Conduct three informational interviews with professionals in different careers within six months.	Schedule meetings, prepare questions, and take notes on career paths.
Research and shortlist three potential career paths within six months.	Use career exploration tools, take assessments, and interview professionals.
Apply for at least five scholarships or financial aid opportunities before the next school year.	Research scholarships, complete applications, and submit required documents.
Maintain a digital or physical planner with all school, work, and personal appointments for three months.	Set reminders and check the planner daily to stay organized.
Vocational Goals	
SMART Goal	**Activity**
Complete a job shadowing experience in a field of interest within six months.	Contact businesses, set up a shadowing day, and observe professionals at work.
Apply for at least two internships or apprenticeships within the next year.	Research opportunities, prepare application materials, and submit applications.
Write and revise a resume and cover letter within the next two months.	Attend a resume-writing workshop and create a polished job application.
Complete at least three mock job interviews within four months.	Practice answering common questions with a mentor, teacher, or career coach.
Apply for at least three part-time jobs or volunteer positions within six months.	Search for job postings, submit applications, and attend interviews.
Learn how to file a simple tax return before tax season next year.	Attend a financial literacy workshop and practice completing a tax form.
Advocate for personal needs at least three times in academic, work, or social settings within three months.	Practice self-advocacy by requesting accommodations, asking for help, or explaining needs.

(*Continued*)

Table 9.1 (continued)

Independent Living Goals	
SMART Goal	**Activity**
Open a bank account and deposit at least $50 within the first month.	Visit a bank, set up an account, and make the first deposit.
Create and follow a budget for three months, tracking all income and expenses.	Use a budgeting app or spreadsheet to log and review expenses weekly.
Plan and prepare three balanced meals per week for the next two months.	Research recipes, create a shopping list, and cook meals independently.
Learn to cook five different meals within two months.	Follow recipes, practice cooking techniques, and get feedback from family or friends.
Change a tire and check oil levels within the next three months.	Watch instructional videos, practice with a mentor, and test your skills on a real car.
Use public transportation to travel to three different locations independently within the next month.	Plan routes using transit maps, purchase tickets, and complete practice trips.
Do laundry once per week for the next three months.	Sort clothes, use a washer/dryer, and fold/hang clothes after washing.
Create and follow a weekly cleaning routine for at least two months.	Assign specific cleaning tasks to each day and track progress.
Arrive on time to at least 90% of commitments (school, work, and appointments) for three months.	Use alarms, reminders, and schedules to manage time effectively.
Understand how to sign a lease and manage utilities before renting an apartment.	Research lease agreements, set up utility accounts, and learn tenant rights.
Health Care/Mental Health Goals	
SMART Goal	**Activity**
Schedule and attend at least two medical appointments in the next six months.	Research providers, call to book appointments, and record dates in a planner.
Learn basic stress management techniques and practice them weekly for three months.	Try meditation, deep breathing, journaling, or physical activity.
Meet with a mental health professional at least once to discuss stress management strategies.	Research local providers, schedule an appointment, and attend the session.
Develop a sleep routine and track sleep patterns for one month.	Set a bedtime schedule, limit screen time before bed, and track sleep quality.

to the plan or provide additional support as needed (Kelly, 2011). Regular meetings are held to discuss the student's progress, celebrate successes, and address challenges. This dynamic approach ensures that the transition plan remains relevant and effective, guiding the student toward a fulfilling and successful adult life and fostering their independence and self-sufficiency. Typically, these meetings are most effective when all participants have a strong understanding of the youth's strengths, needs, goals, and wishes. To accomplish this, you must stick to the guiding principles and ask questions (see Figure 9.2).

Sam began by validating Jessica's anxieties about leaving high school. Beyond entering the next step in her educational journey, Jessica's anxieties also stem from her uncertainty about her placement after she turns 18. Jessica is unsure of the role her foster parents will play as she becomes a legal adult. Sam emphasized her self-determination and agency in the transition

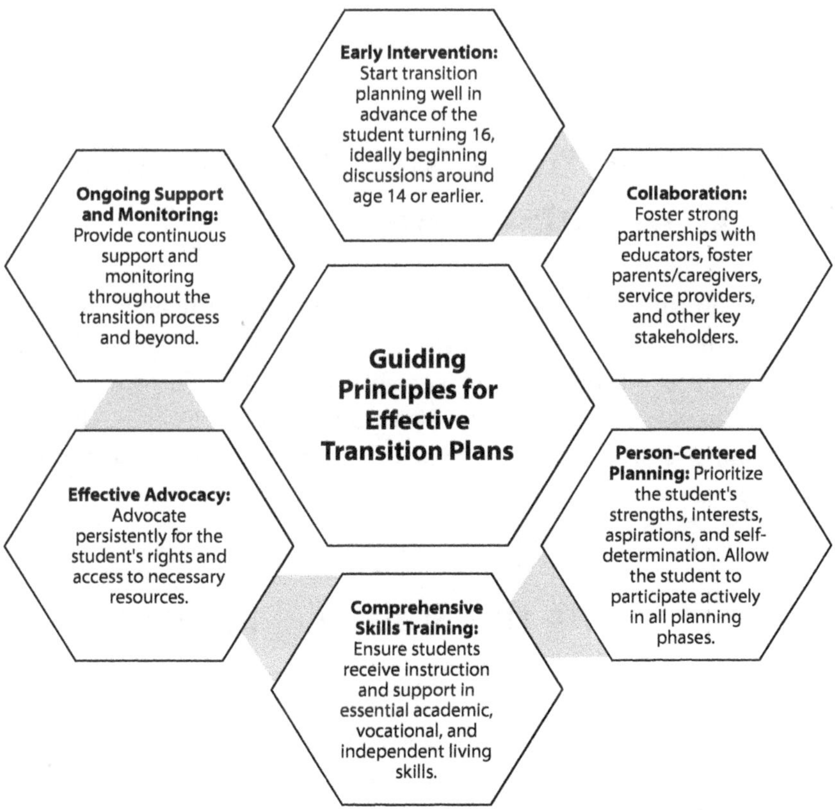

Figure 9.2. Guiding principles for effective transitions.

planning process, reassuring Jessica that her goals would be attainable with the right support. Sam reminds Jessica that her special education transition plan will be similar to the independent living plan that they just completed together through their local Department of Family Services. The first step involves completing a comprehensive assessment, which includes evaluating her academic, vocational, social-emotional, and independent living skills. Sam shares with Jessica that while this assessment sounds daunting, it is generally no more nerve-wracking than filling out a survey or questionnaire. Recognizing that Jessica had experienced significant trauma throughout her life in foster care, Sam checks with the school team to verify that the assessment is trauma-informed, creating a safe and comfortable environment for Jessica to share her experiences and aspirations. The assessment confirmed Jessica's considerable artistic talent, which was already displayed in several local art shows. However, it also highlighted considerable gaps in her independent living skills; she required support with budgeting, cooking, and accessing community resources.

What Questions Should I Ask in a Transition Planning Meeting?

Effective transition planning hinges on thoughtful discussions that take into account the student's unique circumstances and needs. The following groups of questions help prompt a useful dialogue that pinpoints unique needs and aspirations, the family or caregiver's role in the child's life and transition, and the available services and supports needed to develop an effective transition plan.

Understanding the Student's Individual Needs and Aspirations

This section focuses on gathering a comprehensive understanding of the student's unique characteristics, strengths, and aspirations, which form the cornerstone of person-centered planning (Wehmeyer, 2009).

The questions should aim to illuminate their perspectives, goals, and preferences, actively promoting their self-determination and agency. Key areas to explore include:

- **Strengths and Interests:** What are the student's inherent strengths, talents, and skills? What activities genuinely interest them? This information helps identify potential career pathways and leisure pursuits that could enhance their quality of life. Exploring these early provides valuable insights into the student's potential and promotes a strengths-based approach to planning.
- **Current Skills (Academic, Vocational, Independent Living):** What is the student's current level of academic achievement in core subjects? Do they possess any vocational skills (e.g., from part-time jobs, volunteer experience, or extracurricular activities)? What is their current level of independent living skills (e.g., personal care, household management, financial literacy)? Understanding proficiency with these skills forms a crucial baseline for assessing progress.
- **Social-Emotional and Mental Health Needs:** How is the student's emotional well-being? Are there any signs of anxiety, depression, or other mental health concerns? What is the nature of their social interactions and relationships? Understanding these aspects is crucial for developing a supportive and inclusive transition plan, which may require referrals to mental health professionals or other suitable support services.
- **Health and Medical Needs:** What are the youth's current health and medical needs? Are there any ongoing medical conditions or requirements (e.g., medications, therapies)? Are there any physical limitations that need to be considered when planning for future employment or independent living? This information is crucial to preparing for continued healthcare access and any necessary accommodations.
- **Post-School Goals (Education, Employment, Independent Living):** What are the student's aspirations for their future? What are their long-term goals regarding education (e.g., college, vocational training, apprenticeships)? What are their career aspirations and desired employment settings? What are their preferred living arrangements (e.g., independent living, supported living, group

home)? These aspirations provide the framework for establishing SMART goals. The questions should be open-ended, encouraging students to articulate their vision for the future and actively promoting their self-determination.

Understanding the Family/Caregiver's Role and Perspective

For many students, family support is a critical component of a successful transition. However, for youth in foster care, this aspect requires special attention, emphasizing the unique challenges presented by instability and the absence of a traditional family structure. The questions in this section must be sensitive and respectful, acknowledging the complexities and potential challenges faced by foster families. Key aspects to explore include:

- **Understanding and Goals for the Student's Future:** What are the family's (or foster family's) understanding of and aspirations for the student's future? Do they share the student's vision, and are there any potential conflicts or differing perspectives? This line of inquiry explores the alignment between the student's goals and those of their caregivers.
- **Level of Available Support:** What level of support can the family realistically provide? This question is especially crucial for youth in foster care, acknowledging the variability in the support foster families can offer. It assesses their capability to assist the student with tasks such as transportation, financial management, and accessing community resources.
- **Specific Concerns and Challenges:** What are the family's specific concerns and challenges regarding the transition process? This is an open-ended question designed to identify and address any potential obstacles or barriers that could hinder the student's success. For youth in foster care, common concerns may include uncertainty about future housing arrangements, concerns about the student's ability to manage finances independently, and anxieties surrounding their emotional and social well-being after leaving the structured environment of the foster care system.

- **Foster Care History and System Involvement:** For students in foster care, understanding their history within the system is vital. This history might include the number of prior placements, the reasons for placement changes, and the level of support received from the child welfare system. This information provides context and identifies potential challenges that need to be addressed in the transition plan. The child welfare worker plays a key role here, providing valuable insights into the student's history and advocating for their needs within the system.

Assessing Available Services and Supports

Various services and supports are available to youth with disabilities in the child welfare system to ensure they have the opportunity to transition successfully. Services to consider include the following:

- **Educational Services:** What educational options are available (e.g., vocational/trade schools, community colleges, apprenticeships, supported education programs)? What financial aid or support services are available to help the student access these opportunities?
- **Vocational Services:** What vocational training programs and job placement services are available? Are there any supported employment models that could help the student secure and maintain employment?
- **Independent Living Services:** What supports are available to assist the student in developing essential independent living skills? Are there any programs providing instruction in areas such as budgeting, cooking, cleaning, personal care, accessing transportation, and navigating community resources? Are there any organizations providing support in finding housing and establishing independent living arrangements? This section ensures that the transition plan considers the student's holistic needs.
- **Healthcare and Mental Health Services:** What healthcare providers and services are available in the community? What is the plan for transferring medical and mental health records to new providers? How will insurance coverage be ensured for the student? This section addresses the critical need for maintaining continuity of healthcare and mental health support.

Developing a Comprehensive Transition Plan

There are several steps to develop an effective, detailed, and realistic transition plan that adequately prepares youth for success. Consider the following:

- **Specific Steps for Achieving Post-School Goals:** What precise steps are needed to achieve each established goal? This section outlines the action plan, specifying the steps required to achieve the SMART goals. This process involves detailing the timelines for completing educational programs, starting job searches, obtaining appropriate housing, and accessing necessary support services.
- **Realistic Timeline for Achieving Goals:** What is the anticipated timeline for achieving each goal? This section outlines the timeframe for each step. It needs to be realistic, taking into account potential obstacles and challenges.
- **Progress Monitoring Strategies:** How will the student's progress be monitored and evaluated? This step outlines the mechanisms used to track progress toward the goals, including data collection methods, the frequency of monitoring, and procedures for making adjustments as needed.
- **Responsibilities and Accountability:** Who is responsible for each component of the plan? Answers to this question will clarify the roles and responsibilities of each stakeholder, promoting accountability and clear lines of communication.
- **Contingency Planning:** What potential challenges might arise, and what contingency plans are in place to address them? This proactive step identifies potential obstacles (e.g., changes in placement, financial difficulties, health issues) and develops proactive strategies to mitigate their impact.

By addressing these questions thoroughly, the transition planning meeting generates a comprehensive, individualized, and effective transition plan that truly empowers the student to achieve their goals. This person-centered approach fosters self-determination and sets the stage for a successful and fulfilling journey into adulthood.

The next step in Jessica's transition plan was to convene the transition planning team. The school team recently invited Jessica, her foster parents, her special education teacher, a vocational rehabilitation counselor, and a representative from the local mental health agency to a transition meeting. The team's diversity ensures comprehensive coverage of Jessica's needs. Sam asks Jessica if there is anyone else she thinks should be invited, and Jessica replies that she cannot think of anyone else. The meeting started with a discussion of Jessica's goals. Her desire to attend art school was a central part of the transition plan. The team collaboratively mapped out the steps required: completing high school, securing financial aid and scholarships, locating appropriate housing near the art school, and accessing ongoing mental health support for her anxiety. Sam relayed that some funding was available through the state to supplement Jessica's tuition and living expenses. They worked together to craft SMART goals, establishing concrete, measurable objectives with specific timelines. For example, Jessica

The team also identified and allocated necessary supports. Jessica's special education teacher was committed to providing additional academic support to help her graduate. The vocational rehabilitation counselor agreed to help her secure financial aid and scholarships and explore potential apprenticeships at local art studios. Sam, acutely aware of Jessica's history of trauma and instability, ensured she received ongoing support from the local mental health agency, emphasizing the importance of continuity of services. Sam also committed to regular check-ins with Jessica and her foster parents, providing consistent support and advocating for their needs within the child welfare system. They discussed potential challenges and proactively developed contingency plans, including strategies to address potential housing instability or disruptions in her foster care placement. Jessica committed to the plan and agreed to reach out to each other's stakeholders at least once per month or when in need of guidance.

How Can I Help Youth Transition Effectively into a New Placement, School, or Post-Secondary Opportunity?

Successfully navigating the transition from secondary school to post-secondary opportunities is a significant milestone for many young people. Still, it presents unique and often formidable challenges for youth with disabilities in foster care. These challenges are amplified by the instability inherent in their lives, including frequent changes in placement, inconsistent access to essential support services, and, too often, a lack of consistent guidance from a supportive family. Therefore, effective transition planning requires a multifaceted, proactive approach that extends across all aspects of the young person's life. Furthermore, it is important to recognize that transition can take several forms. Beyond post-secondary transitions, situations may arise in which students transition from placements, schools, grade levels, or classrooms. All of these transitions can cause stress and disturbance. Regardless of the type of transition, limiting disruptions and maintaining continuity of care and services is paramount. These outcomes can be achieved by focusing on several overarching objectives.

Build Strong Collaborative Partnerships

Effective transition support demands a collaborative team effort, bringing together a range of professionals and the young person themselves. This team includes special and general education teachers, school counselors, therapists, and related service providers, such as occupational therapists, physical therapists, speech-language therapists, child welfare workers, vocational rehabilitation counselors, healthcare providers, and, critically, the young person and their family or legal guardians. Open communication and consistent sharing of information are essential. Regular meetings, whether formal IEP meetings or informal check-ins, ensure that everyone remains informed and aligned toward the same objective: the young person's success. The child welfare worker plays a pivotal role, facilitating these interactions, advocating for the young person's needs, and ensuring continuity of care across all settings. Building strong, trusting relationships between team members is critical to the plan's effectiveness.

Employ a Trauma-Informed Approach

Many youth in foster care have experienced significant trauma (see Chapter 6), potentially impacting their ability to participate fully in the transition planning process due to their capacity to manage change.

A trauma-informed approach acknowledges the profound impact of trauma and emphasizes practices that prioritize safety, trust, choice, collaboration, and empowerment (SAMHSA's National Child Traumatic Stress Network, n.d.). This approach involves creating a supportive and nonjudgmental environment where the young person feels safe sharing their experiences and concerns. Consider that youth in foster care may be used to unwelcome changes being thrust upon them; as such, they may struggle to share or even consider their wishes or post-secondary desires. Strategies might encourage open communication, including active listening, validating their feelings, and providing choices whenever possible. Trauma-informed practices extend to all interactions, from planning meetings to service provision, creating a consistent, supportive experience.

Implement Person-Centered Planning and Promote Self-Determination

Transition planning must be truly person-centered, prioritizing the young person's self-determination, strengths, and aspirations (Wehmeyer, 2009). This means actively involving them in every stage of the process, from the initial assessment to setting goals and selecting services. The plan should not be imposed upon them; it should reflect their unique needs, interests, and vision for their future. Even so, resources such as formal and informal assessments will prove valuable in guiding their thoughts and any discussion. A person-centered approach fosters a sense of ownership and control, empowering them to make informed decisions about their lives. Open-ended questions and active listening are essential for understanding their perspectives and preferences.

Ensuring Continuity of Care Across Placements

The instability inherent in the foster care system, such as frequent changes in placement, can disrupt educational progress and access to consistent services. To mitigate this, proactive strategies are critical. These strategies include maintaining open communication with schools and service providers across placements, meticulous record-keeping to ensure a complete picture of the young person's history and needs, and close collaboration among all stakeholders to maintain continuity of care. As a child welfare worker, you may have the most background knowledge of the child's needs and educational history. As such, you will prove to be a valuable source of information for all stakeholders, as well as the knowledge needed to be a strong advocate. Advocating for consistent access to essential services, such as therapy, education, and healthcare, throughout any placement changes is crucial. Furthermore, employing trauma-informed practices creates a supportive environment that fosters the young person's emotional well-being during these transitions.

Supporting Successful School Transitions

Transitions within the school system, such as moving between schools, grade levels, or classrooms, can also be disruptive. To ensure a smooth transition, collaborate closely with school administrators and teachers to facilitate the transfer of educational records, introduce the child to new teachers and staff, and advocate for any necessary accommodations. Allow the child ample time to familiarize themselves with their new environment before the transition. Finally, maintain consistent communication channels between the school, the family (or foster family), and service providers to monitor the child's progress and address any challenges that arise.

Facilitate Access to Post-secondary Opportunities

As we have explained, the transition to post-secondary education or employment requires significant preparation. Begin exploring post-secondary options well in advance of high school graduation, allowing ample time for research, gathering information on available programs, understanding funding opportunities, and preparing for the transition. Ensure the youth has access to career counseling and vocational assessments to help the student identify their interests and suitable career paths. Additionally, if relevant, consider how the student's foster care transition plan overlaps with the special education transition plan. Assist in securing post-secondary opportunities, such as college, vocational school, apprenticeship, or supported employment program, and ensure access to support services (e.g., tutoring, mentoring, financial aid, assistive technology). Provide access to instruction and support in developing essential independent living skills, such as budgeting, cooking, cleaning, personal care, transportation, and community resources to prepare the student for life beyond the structured school environment. Partner with vocational rehabilitation agencies for support in securing and maintaining employment. If the young person is aging out of the foster care system, explore and assist with establishing legal guardianship, if needed, to safeguard their well-being and continued support.

The ultimate result in Jessica's case was a comprehensive, person-centered transition plan built on collaboration and emphasizing her self-determination. It addressed not only her educational and career goals but also her social-emotional well-being and independent living skills. This plan offered a clear roadmap to a more stable future, acknowledging the challenges Jessica had overcome and preparing her for future possibilities. Sam's ongoing role will be critical to ensuring the plan remains responsive to her evolving needs and provides consistent support throughout her transition. Sam also knows that not every special education transition plan will be this straightforward, but she feels confident that she understands the process and is relieved that there is a plan in place to support Jessica.

Formal transition planning ends when the IEP concludes. One year before the youth reaches the age of majority, which is typically 18 in most states, the IEP team should begin preparing the youth to make their own education decisions. Once the youth reaches the age of majority, they will gain the decision-making rights previously held by their parents and guardians, including the ability to decide if their parents or caregivers will attend IEP meetings, whether to consent to evaluations, and to approve changes in services or placements. A guardianship process may be initiated if the youth is unable to manage these rights and responsibilities. Otherwise, special education services can continue for a student until they earn a standard or advanced high school diploma or reach the age of 22. Although formal special education transition planning has concluded at this point, support for youth with disabilities likely continues in other forms. As a child welfare worker, you should continue to monitor the youth's progress toward achieving their goals and aspirations and seek resources to support them.

Where Can I Find More Information About Transition Plans and Post-Secondary Transition?

- **Document:** *A Transition Guide to Post-secondary Education and Employment for Students and Youth with Disabilities*

  Published by the U.S. Department of Education's Office of Special Education and Rehabilitative Services (OSERS), this guide provides insights into the transition process, covering education and employment options, as well as strategies to support youth with disabilities in achieving their post-secondary goals. https://www.ed.gov/sites/ed/files/about/offices/list/osers/transition/products/postsecondary-transition-guide-08–2020.pdf

- **Center:** *National Technical Assistance Center on Transition (NTACT)*

  NTACT provides resources and information on effective practices for youth with disabilities as they transition from school to post-secondary education and employment. Their materials include toolkits, webinars, and research-based strategies to enhance transition planning. https://transitionta.org/category/resource/training/

- **Module:** *The IRIS Center at Vanderbilt University*

  This IRIS Center Module helps participants understand secondary transition. Topics include the school counselor's role, transition assessments, preparing for postsecondary education and employment, and referral to outside agencies. These resources are designed to enhance the knowledge and skills of those involved in transition planning. https://iris.peabody.vanderbilt.edu/module/tran/

- **Organization:** *Casey Family Programs.*

  This organization provides strategies and advocacy to enhance educational outcomes for children in foster care, including those who have disabilities. Take a look at their resources, including formal and informal assessments. https://www.casey.org/resources/practice-tools/

References

Bateman, B. D. (2017). Individualized education programs. In J. M. Kauffman & D. P. Hallahan (Eds.), *Handbook of special education* (2nd ed., pp. 91–124). Taylor & Francis.

Gershwin, T. (2022). Building and maintaining trusting and equitable partnerships with families. In A. Turnbull, H. R. Turnbull, G. L. Francis, M. Burke, K. Kyzar, S. J. Haines, T. Gershwin, K. G. Shepherd, N. Holdren, & G. H. S. Singer (Eds.), *Families and professionals: Trusting partnerships in general and special education* (8th ed., pp. 852–867). Pearson.

Hedin, L., & DeSpain, S. (2018). SMART or not? Writing specific, measurable IEP goals. *Teaching Exceptional Children, 51*(2), 100–110. http://dx.doi.org/10.1177/0040059918802587

Individuals with Disabilities Education Act of 2004, 20 U.S.C. § 1400.

IRIS Center. (n.d.). *Secondary transition: Interagency collaboration.* Vanderbilt University. https://iris.peabody.vanderbilt.edu/module/tran/

Kelly, K. (2011, August). *Education transition plans for children in foster care.* ABA Child Law Practice. https://ittakesanohana.org/wp-content/uploads/2011/08/Transition-Plans-CLP.pdf

Rossetti, Z., Redash, A., Sauer, J. S., Bui, O., Wen, Y., & Regensburger, D. (2020). Access, accountability, and advocacy: Culturally and linguistically diverse families' participation in IEP meetings. *Exceptionality, 28*(3), 148–160. https://doi.org/10.1080/09362835.2018.1480948

Substance Abuse and Mental Health Services Administration. (n.d.). *National child traumatic stress initiative (NCTSI).* https://www.samhsa.gov/mental-health/trauma-violence/nctsi

Wehmeyer, M. L. (2009). *Self-determination and the education of students with disabilities.* Paul H Brookes Publishing.

10

Navigating Disagreements and Fostering Consensus in IEP Teams

As we have described in prior chapters, the creation and implementation of an Individualized Education Program (IEP) stands as a cornerstone of special education, mandated by the Individuals with Disabilities Education Act (IDEA) to ensure that children with disabilities receive a free and appropriate public education (FAPE) tailored to their unique needs (Yell et al., 2021). This process involves convening a multidisciplinary team, bringing together the expertise and perspectives of parents or caregivers, educators, related service providers, school administrators, and, when appropriate, the child themselves. While the ultimate aim of this collaboration is to develop a comprehensive and effective educational plan, the diverse viewpoints, professional responsibilities, and deeply held beliefs of team members can inevitably lead to disagreements (Fish, 2008).

This chapter delves into the multifaceted nature of disagreements within IEP teams, recognizing them not necessarily as failures of the process but rather as potential opportunities for deeper understanding and more robust decision-making. The following sections will explore the common sources of these disagreements, emphasizing the distinct perspectives brought by different team members, including child welfare workers. Additionally, we will examine proactive strategies for fostering open communication and building trust, as well as specific techniques for navigating difficult conversations and reaching a consensus that prioritizes the child's best interests. Finally, we will outline the formal and informal dispute-resolution processes available when consensus proves elusive, underscoring the importance of understanding these mechanisms for effective advocacy. In doing so, we will answer the following questions:

1. What are the unique perspectives of IEP team members?
2. What are some common areas of disagreement among IEP team members?
3. What are some proactive strategies for fostering open communication and trust?
4. What are some strategies for navigating disagreements and reaching a consensus?
5. What are formal and informal dispute-resolution procedures?
6. Where can I find more information about navigating disagreements in special education?

What Are the Unique Perspectives of IEP Team Members?

Disagreements within IEP teams can stem from a complex interplay of factors rooted in differing perspectives, values, data interpretations, and resource considerations. Recognizing these potential sources of disagreement begins with perspective-taking, or the ability to see different points of view or ways of looking at a topic (Trainor, 2010).

The Perspective of Parents and Caregivers

Parents, whether biological, adoptive, or foster, bring a unique depth of knowledge about their child's history, strengths, needs, and preferences. Parents or caregivers often possess a long-term perspective and a profound emotional investment in their child's well-being and educational success (Burke et al., 2016). Disagreements may arise when parents feel their insights are not adequately valued, when they have concerns about the proposed goals or services, or when they perceive a mismatch between the school's assessment of their child's needs and their own lived experiences. Furthermore, parents may feel overwhelmed by the technical jargon and procedures of special education, which can lead to feelings of marginalization and a sense of power imbalance with educational professionals (Lake & Billingsley, 2000). For foster parents, their role, while crucial, may be further complicated by legal limitations or a lack of complete information regarding the child's history. Child welfare workers can play a vital role in ensuring the voices of these caregivers are heard and respected. Their understanding of family dynamics can provide crucial context for the educational team. Moreover, child welfare workers often have a broader understanding of the systemic factors affecting the child's education and what external support may be required beyond the school setting. They are uniquely positioned to help caregivers navigate complex systems and explain the child's needs to education professionals.

The Perspective of Educational Professionals

Educators, including general and special education teachers, school psychologists, and related service providers (such as speech therapists and occupational therapists), bring specialized knowledge of child development, learning theories, assessment practices, and evidence-based interventions. Their perspective is often shaped by their professional training, experience with a diverse range of students, and an understanding of the curriculum and available school-based resources. Disagreements may occur when educators believe parental expectations are unrealistic, when they have concerns about the feasibility of implementing certain interventions within the school setting, or when they must balance the needs of an individual student with those of the broader classroom or school system. Budgetary constraints, staffing limitations, such as a shortage of service providers and specialists, unmanageable workloads, and district policies can also influence their recommendations and contribute to disagreements.

The Unique Role of the Child Welfare Worker

Child welfare workers, including social workers and Court Appointed Special Advocates (CASAs), occupy a unique position within the IEP team. Their primary focus is on the holistic well-being of the child, considering not only their educational needs but also their safety, permanency, and social-emotional development (Fraser, 2004). Child welfare workers bring a broader systemic perspective, understanding the impact of trauma, placement instability, and family dynamics on the child's learning and behavior. Disagreements may arise when the educational recommendations do not adequately address the child's trauma history, when there are concerns about the stability or appropriateness of the educational placement in relation to the child's living situation, or when the child welfare worker believes that additional external supports and services are necessary for the child's educational success. Their advocacy often extends beyond ensuring compliance with educational legalities to coordinating necessary resources and support services. Child welfare workers act as advocates for the child, especially when the child's voice might not be fully heard or understood.

Ms. Brown, a child welfare worker, is attending the annual IEP review meeting for ten-year-old Isaac, who was diagnosed with an emotional disturbance and a specific learning disability. The meeting includes Ms. Rodriguez, the special education teacher; Mr. Davis, the general education teacher; and Ms. Lee, the school psychologist. Isaac's foster parent, Ms. Evans, is also present and voices concerns about Isaac's lack of progress in reading despite receiving two 30-minute sessions of specialized reading instruction per week. Ms. Rodriguez presents data showing minimal gains in Isaac's reading fluency and comprehension over the past year, attributing this to his emotional regulation challenges, which often led to his disengagement during instruction. Mr. Davis echoes these sentiments, noting that Isaac struggled to keep up with grade-level reading material in his general education classes, impacting his understanding of other subjects. Ms. Lee highlighted Isaac's ongoing difficulties with anxiety and social skills, suggesting that his emotional state significantly interfered with his learning. Ms. Evans expressed her frustration, stating, "It just doesn't seem like he's getting enough help. He comes home feeling defeated because he can't read what the other kids are reading. We try to work with him at home, but it is a constant struggle, and he gets so upset."

What Are Some Common Areas of Disagreement Among IEP Team Members?

Evaluation and Eligibility

The process of evaluating a child for special education services and determining eligibility based on one of the thirteen disability categories recognized by IDEA can also be a significant source of disagreement. Parents or caregivers may disagree with the evaluation findings, believing their child has a disability that was not identified or that the severity of the disability was underestimated. Conversely, school personnel may find that the child does not meet the eligibility criteria or that the child's academic or behavioral challenges are primarily due to factors other than a disability, such as a lack of appropriate instruction or attendance issues. Disagreements can also arise regarding the appropriateness of the evaluation tools and procedures, particularly concerns about nondiscriminatory evaluation practices. IDEA mandates that evaluations be comprehensive and nondiscriminatory to ensure accurate identification of a child's needs (Zirkel, 2020).

The Contents of the IEP

After eligibility is established, disagreements can emerge during the development of the IEP document. These may involve:

- Present Levels of Academic Achievement and Functional Performance (PLAAFP): Parents or other team members may disagree with the school's description of the child's current strengths and needs. This section forms the foundation of the IEP, and differing perceptions of the child's abilities can lead to disagreements about what are considered appropriate goals and services.
- Measurable Annual Goals: There may be differing opinions on the appropriateness, ambitiousness, or measurability of the proposed goals. Ensuring goals are Specific, Measurable, Attainable, Relevant, and Time-bound (SMART), as discussed in Chapter 5, can help

mitigate these disagreements. Ambiguous or unrealistic goals can hinder progress monitoring and create further conflict.

- Special Education and Related Services: Disagreements can arise regarding the type, frequency, intensity, and delivery of special education and related services, such as counseling, occupational therapy, and speech therapy. Parents may advocate for more intensive or different types of services than the school deems necessary or feasible. Related services are crucial for supporting a child's ability to benefit from special education.
- Supplementary Aids and Services: The need for any supplementary aids and services (e.g., assistive technology, paraprofessional support) can also be a point of contention. These supports are intended to enable the child to be educated with nondisabled peers to the maximum extent appropriate.
- Least Restrictive Environment (LRE): Determining the most appropriate least restrictive environment where the child can be educated to the maximum extent appropriate with nondisabled peers can be a significant area of disagreement. Parents or caregivers often advocate for either more inclusive settings or more individualized support. As mentioned throughout this book, IDEA emphasizes educating children with disabilities in the least restrictive environment (LRE).
- Progress Monitoring: Disagreements may occur regarding how the child's progress toward their goals will be measured and reported. Clear and consistent progress monitoring is essential for determining the effectiveness of the IEP and making necessary adjustments.

What Are Some Proactive Strategies for Fostering Open Communication and Trust?

Recognizing the differing perspectives and Ms. Evans's clear dissatisfaction, Ms. Brown employed active listening and perspective-taking. "Ms. Evans, could you tell us more about what you see at home when Isaac tries to do his reading homework?" she asked, aiming to gain a deeper understanding of the challenges beyond the school setting. Ms. Evans described Isaac's avoidance behaviors, his expressions of feeling "stupid," and the significant time and emotional energy required to get him to engage in reading tasks. Ms. Brown then turned to Ms. Rodriguez, saying, "Ms. Rodriguez, considering what Ms. Evans has shared and the limited progress data, have you considered any alternative or more intensive reading interventions that might better address Isaac's specific learning disability in conjunction with his emotional needs?" Ms. Rodriguez mentioned the school's structured literacy program but indicated that it was only offered in the same small group format Isaac was currently receiving. Mr. Davis expressed concerns about the feasibility of providing more individualized reading support within the constraints of his general education classroom. Ms. Lee suggested that Isaac's anxiety might be a barrier to learning and proposed increasing his counseling sessions. However, Ms. Brown gently refocused the conversation on reading instruction, stating, "While Isaac's emotional well-being is paramount, and the counseling is important, let's ensure we're also exploring all avenues to address his reading deficits directly. Perhaps a more intensive, individualized reading intervention, possibly even short-term, could help him build foundational skills and increase his confidence, which in turn might positively impact his emotional state."

Preventing disagreements from escalating into intractable conflicts begins with establishing a foundation of open communication and mutual trust among all IEP team members. Proactive strategies can cultivate an environment where diverse perspectives are valued, norms are upheld, concerns are addressed early, and collaborative problem-solving is prioritized.

Initiating Early and Frequent Communication

Rather than waiting for the formal IEP meeting, initiating communication early in the process can help preempt potential disagreements. Child welfare workers can reach out to the school team to share relevant information about the child's background and current circumstances, as well as to understand the school's initial assessment and proposed interventions. Similarly, fostering open lines of communication between the school and the foster parents or other caregivers ensures that everyone is kept informed and has the opportunity to voice their perspectives before decisions are finalized. Regular informal check-ins, in addition to formal meetings, can help build rapport and address emerging concerns before they become major points of contention. Preemptive communication can establish priorities and open productive dialogue.

Establishing Clear Communication Norms

Establishing clear norms for communication during meetings at the outset of the IEP process can be beneficial. These norms include agreeing to listen respectfully to all viewpoints without interruption, using straightforward and jargon-free language, and focusing on the child's needs as the central priority. The examples of collaborative language provided in Chapter 4 offer valuable guidance in fostering a positive and productive communication environment. Encouraging all participants to express their thoughts and concerns openly and honestly while also being mindful of time constraints is crucial.

Sharing Information and Data Transparently

Ensuring that all IEP team members have access to relevant evaluation data, progress monitoring reports, and other pertinent information in a timely manner can help promote shared understanding and reduce the likelihood of disagreements based on incomplete or misinterpreted information. Child welfare workers can assist caregivers in understanding complex evaluation results and can also share relevant information from the child welfare system that may have implications for the child's education. Transparency in sharing information fosters trust and allows for more informed and collaborative decision-making. Understanding the data and evidence used to support recommendations can help move the conversation away from subjective opinions.

What Are Some Strategies for Navigating Disagreements and Reaching Consensus?

To move toward consensus, Ms. Brown proposed a collaborative problem-solving approach. "What if we explored the possibility of temporarily increasing Isaac's direct, individualized reading instruction with a specialist for a set period, say, eight weeks, and then closely monitor his progress?" she suggested. "We could also look into incorporating some of the calming techniques Ms. Lee uses in her counseling sessions into the reading instruction to help Isaac manage any anxiety that arises." Ms. Rodriguez was initially hesitant due to staffing constraints, but agreed to explore the availability of additional reading support resources within the district. Mr. Davis offered to collaborate with the reading specialist to reinforce newly learned skills in the general education setting. Ms. Lee supported this integrated approach, emphasizing the potential positive impact of improved reading skills on Isaac's overall confidence and emotional well-being. Ms. Evans expressed relief and hope that a more intensive approach could finally help Isaac make meaningful progress. Before concluding the meeting, Ms. Brown summarized the agreed-upon action items: exploring options for increased individualized reading instruction, integrating calming techniques into reading sessions, and a follow-up meeting in eight weeks to review Isaac's progress. By proactively addressing the foster parents' concerns, facilitating open communication, and focusing on the child's best interests through a data-informed and flexible approach, Ms. Brown helped the IEP team reach a consensus on a revised plan that more directly addressed Isaac's critical needs.

Despite proactive communication efforts, disagreements will inevitably arise. Approaching these difficult conversations with a focus on constructive dialogue and collaborative problem-solving is essential for reaching a consensus that effectively addresses the child's needs. Conversations may not appear as straightforward as those presented in this vignette; however, using the following strategies should help you get closer to a resolution in the vast majority of disagreements.

Active Listening and Perspective-Taking

When disagreements surface, practicing active listening is paramount. Active listening involves paying close attention to what others say, both verbally and nonverbally, asking clarifying questions to ensure understanding, and acknowledging their perspectives, even if you do not agree with them. Using the strategies from Chapter 5 can be helpful in this task. Encouraging all team members to consider the situation from different viewpoints, including the parent's concerns about their child's well-being, the teacher's insights into classroom dynamics, the related service provider's clinical expertise, and the child welfare worker's understanding of the child's broader context can help identify common ground and potential solutions.

Focusing on the Child's Best Interests

The overarching principle guiding all IEP team discussions should be in the child's best interests. When disagreements arise, revisiting this central focus can help team members prioritize and find solutions that truly benefit the student. Child welfare workers, with their holistic view of the child's well-being, can play a key role in ensuring this perspective remains central.

Utilizing Data and Evidence

Grounding discussions in objective data, such as evaluation results, progress monitoring data, and evidence-based interventions, can move the conversation away from subjective opinions and toward more informed decision-making. Child welfare workers can advocate for considering information related to the child's trauma history and its potential impact on learning and behavior.

Exploring Alternative Solutions and Compromise

Reaching consensus often requires a willingness from all team members to be flexible and to explore alternative solutions. Brainstorming different approaches, considering the potential benefits and drawbacks of each option, and being open to compromise can lead to creative and effective solutions that address the concerns of all parties while prioritizing the child's needs. Phrases like "Let's explore that further together" or "What other supports might be beneficial?" can encourage a collaborative problem-solving approach. Identifying areas of agreement can also help build consensus.

Practicing Patience and Respectful Communication

Navigating disagreements can sometimes be a time-consuming process that requires patience and perseverance. Maintaining a respectful tone and avoiding accusatory language, even when strong differences of opinion exist, is crucial for fostering a positive and productive dialogue. Taking a break when emotions become heightened can also be a helpful strategy, allowing team members to regroup and approach the discussion with renewed focus. It may take several meetings to reach a consensus on IEPs, so don't feel pressured to complete the IEP process within a specific timeframe.

Documenting Agreements and Action Items

Once a consensus is reached on specific aspects of the IEP, it is essential to document the agreements clearly, including the specific actions that will be taken, the individuals responsible for those actions, and the agreed-upon timelines. This documentation ensures clarity and accountability and provides a reference point for future discussions and progress monitoring. Additionally, if disagreements persist on certain aspects of the IEP, partial consent can be given on the sections for which parents or caregivers consent. Partial consent can be provided by noting the items to which the parents or caregivers object when signing (see Understood Team, n.d.). Despite efforts to work collaboratively and come to a consensus on key components of the IEP, disagreements between the IEP team sometimes require additional procedural support.

What Are the Formal and Informal Dispute-Resolution Procedures?

Despite best efforts at collaborative problem-solving, situations may arise where the IEP team reaches an impasse and cannot agree on essential components of the IEP. In such cases, it is crucial to be aware of the formal and informal dispute-resolution processes available under IDEA.

Informal Resolution

- Further Dialogue and Reconvening the IEP Team: Often, reconvening the IEP prteam for additional discussions, perhaps with a fresh perspective or with more time dedicated to addressing the specific points of disagreement, can lead to resolution.
- IEP Facilitation: Some states offer IEP facilitation, where a neutral third party helps guide the IEP meeting to ensure that all participants can fully and collaboratively participate. This facilitator focuses on the meeting process, not the content, and can be particularly helpful when dealing with complex or controversial issues. IEP facilitation is an early dispute-resolution option not required by IDEA, and its availability varies by state. It can improve relationships among team members and help resolve disagreements more quickly.
- Mediation: Engaging a neutral facilitator or mediator can also be a valuable informal step. A mediator is a trained third party who helps facilitate communication and negotiation between the parties, aiming to reach a mutually agreeable solution. Mediation is a voluntary process and does not involve the mediator imposing a decision on the team. Discussions in mediation are confidential and cannot be used as evidence in a due process hearing or civil lawsuit. The state bears the cost of mediation. A legally binding agreement reached through mediation must be signed by both the parent and an agency representative with the authority to bind the agency.

Formal Resolution

- Resolution Meeting: After a due process complaint is filed, the local educational agency must convene a resolution meeting with the parents and relevant IEP team members within 15 days of receiving the complaint. This meeting provides an opportunity for parents to discuss their complaint and for the agency to resolve it before a due process hearing takes place. The agency must include a representative with decision-making authority. An attorney for the local educational agency cannot attend unless an attorney also accompanies the parent. If a resolution is reached, a legally binding agreement is executed, which can be voided by either party within three business days.
- Due Process Complaint and Hearing: Due process is a formal way to resolve disputes under IDEA. This process begins by filing a written complaint that outlines the dispute and alleges a violation of the IDEA. The complaint must state a violation related to the identification, evaluation, educational placement, or provision of a Free and Appropriate Public Education (FAPE). The party requesting the hearing cannot raise issues not included in the complaint notice unless the other party agrees. A due process hearing is conducted by an impartial hearing officer who is knowledgeable in special education law. A formal record of the hearing is made, and a written decision with findings of fact and conclusions of law is issued. This decision is legally binding and can be appealed in state or federal court. Due process complaints must generally be filed within two years of when the party knew or should have known about the alleged violation.
- State Complaint: Another option is to file a written complaint with the state educational agency if there is a belief that the school has violated IDEA. State complaints can address issues affecting more than just one child and may lead to a state investigation. States have their own rules for handling these complaints, but a written decision must typically be issued within 60 calendar days of receiving the complaint. Unlike due process, state complaints do not necessarily require collaborative resolution efforts.
- Office for Civil Rights (OCR) Complaint: Section 504 of the Rehabilitation Act also protects students with IEPs from

Table 10.1 Dispute-Resolution Pathways in Special Education

Pathway	What It Is	Who Can Initiate?	How a Child Welfare Worker Might Use This Pathway
Informal Problem-Solving / Additional IEP Meeting	Team schedules another IEP meeting (or series of meetings) to review data, clarify concerns, and revise the IEP. This is the least formal option and focuses on relationship-building and collaboration rather than legal procedures.	Any IEP team member (typically the parent/caregiver, foster parent, or school staff) may request another IEP meeting.	Encourage the team to meet again when disagreements emerge, help caregivers prepare questions and priorities, and ensure the child's foster care history and trauma-related needs are clearly explained to the team.
Facilitated IEP Meeting (Where Available)	A trained, neutral facilitator helps guide the IEP meeting, keeps the discussion focused on the student, and supports respectful communication. The facilitator does not take sides or make decisions.	Typically requested by the parent/caregiver or school district through the state education agency, where this option is offered.	Suggest a facilitated IEP when communication has broken down but the team is willing to keep working together. Help caregivers clarify desired outcomes and ground the discussion in data and the child's best interests.

Pathway	What It Is	Who Can Initiate?	How a Child Welfare Worker Might Use This Pathway
Mediation	A voluntary process in which a neutral mediator helps the parent/caregiver and school district resolve disagreements. Mediation is confidential, free to families, and can occur before or after other options (such as filing a complaint). Any agreement is put in writing and is legally binding.	Usually requested jointly by the parent/caregiver and the school district through the state education agency.	Help caregivers understand mediation as a problem-solving approach that is less adversarial than a due process hearing. Support them in identifying specific issues, documenting concerns, and clarifying what acceptable solutions would look like.
State Complaint	A written complaint to the state education agency alleging that the school district has violated federal or state special education requirements (e.g., not implementing the IEP, missing timelines, or denying required services). The state investigates and issues written findings and required corrective actions. This is a **separate process from a due process complaint**, not a hearing.	Any individual or organization (including a child welfare agency or CASA) may file a state complaint, usually about violations that occurred within a specified time period (often the past year, depending on state rules).	Consider this pathway when the issue involves clear noncompliance (e.g., services in the IEP are not being provided). Because it is not a due process complaint, agencies and advocates can use it to address systemic or individual violations. Gather documentation (IEP, progress reports, emails) and, when appropriate, coordinate with the child's attorney or guardian ad litem before filing.

Pathway	What It Is	Who Can Initiate?	How a Child Welfare Worker Might Use This Pathway
Resolution Session (After a Due Process Complaint Is Filed)	A mandatory meeting the district must convene within a short timeline after a parent files a due process complaint. The goal is to resolve the dispute without a hearing. If the parties reach an agreement, they sign a legally binding settlement.	Automatically scheduled by the district after a parent/caregiver files for due process, unless both sides agree in writing to waive the session or use mediation instead.	Help caregivers prepare for this meeting by clarifying non-negotiables and areas where compromise is possible, and by making sure the agreement addresses the child's educational and foster care needs (e.g., stability of placement and school-of-origin issues).
Due Process Hearing	A formal, trial-like procedure before an impartial hearing officer. Both sides present evidence and witnesses, may be represented by attorneys, and receive a written decision. This is the most formal and adversarial option and can be time-consuming and emotionally taxing.	Parents/caregivers (and, in some states, older students) or school districts may file a due process complaint.	Typically, you will not file on your own but may support caregivers or the child's attorney by documenting how educational decisions affect the child's safety, permanency, and well-being. Help ensure trauma history, placement changes, and service gaps are clearly presented as part of the evidence.

Pathway	What It Is	Who Can Initiate?	How a Child Welfare Worker Might Use This Pathway
Section 504 / ADA Complaint to the Office for Civil Rights (OCR)	A written complaint to the U.S. Department of Education's Office for Civil Rights (or a similar agency) alleging disability discrimination or denial of equal access (e.g., failure to provide accommodations, retaliation for advocacy). This process focuses on civil rights, not just IEP content.	Any member of the public may file a complaint within the required timelines.	Consider this pathway when concerns center on discrimination or access (e.g., exclusion from activities or refusal to provide reasonable accommodations), especially for students receiving services under Section 504 rather than IDEA. Coordinate with legal counsel or supervisors in your agency before filing.

discrimination and provides another federal avenue for dispute resolution through a complaint to the Office for Civil Rights (OCR) of the U.S. Department of Education. An OCR complaint must be filed within 180 days of the alleged discrimination. Like state complaints, an OCR complaint may lead to an investigation of the school.

Ideally, strong collaboration and advocacy skills will make any formal dispute-resolution procedures unnecessary or, at a minimum, very rare. Even so, child welfare workers have a responsibility to be aware of these formal dispute-resolution processes and to inform foster parents and other caregivers of their rights under the IDEA if collaborative efforts to reach a consensus are unsuccessful. Understanding these processes empowers caregivers to understand the avenues available to them should intractable differences or a violation of the student's rights occur. Resources such as CADRE (Center for Appropriate Dispute Resolution in Special Education) provide valuable information on dispute-resolution practices (CADRE, 2022).

Maintaining Momentum and Ensuring Effective Implementation

Reaching an agreement on the IEP is a significant milestone, but it is not the end of the collaborative process. Following up regularly after IEP meetings is crucial to ensure that the agreed-upon services and supports are being implemented effectively and that the child is making progress toward their goals. Establishing a timeline for regular check-ins and maintaining open lines of communication among all team members helps ensure accountability and allows for timely adjustments to the IEP if needed. Child welfare workers should actively participate in these follow-up discussions, providing insights into the child's progress in all areas of their life and advocating for any necessary modifications to the IEP based on their observations and the input of caregivers and other service providers. The IEP should not be viewed as a static document but rather as a living plan that is regularly reviewed and revised to reflect the child's evolving needs and progress. Regular meetings and utilizing effective communication strategies are essential for maintaining open lines of communication.

Navigating disagreements within IEP teams is an inherent aspect of the collaborative process envisioned by IDEA. By understanding the diverse perspectives of team members, prioritizing proactive communication, employing strategies for constructive dialogue, and being knowledgeable about dispute-resolution options, IEP teams can effectively work through disagreements and reach a consensus that truly serves the best interests of students with disabilities. Child welfare workers play a vital and unique role in this process, bringing a holistic perspective and advocating tirelessly for the educational and overall well-being of children in the child welfare system. Ultimately, the ability of IEP teams to navigate disagreements constructively and to foster a collaborative environment is fundamental to ensuring that all children with disabilities receive a free and appropriate public education that meets their unique needs and prepares them for future success.

Where Can I Find More Information About Navigating Disagreements and Fostering Consensus in IEP Teams?

- **Organization:** *The Center for Appropriate Dispute Resolution in Special Education (CADRE)*

  CADRE is a nationally recognized center that provides resources and training on effective dispute-resolution practices in special education. Their website offers a wealth of information on mediation, facilitation, and other collaborative approaches to resolving disagreements between families and schools. https://cadreworks.org/for-families

- **Organization:** *Parent Training and Information Centers (PTIs)*

  PTIs are located in every state and provide training and information to parents of children with disabilities. They can offer guidance on navigating the IEP process, understanding parental rights, and advocating effectively for their children's needs. Find your local PTI here: https://www.parentcenterhub.org/find-your-center/

- **Website:** *Wrightslaw*

  Wrightslaw is a website created by special education attorney Pete Wright and his wife, Pam Wright. It provides comprehensive information on special education law, advocacy, and dispute resolution. The site includes articles, cases, and other resources for parents, educators, and advocates. https://www.wrightslaw.com/

- **Organization:** *National Disability Rights Network (NDRN)*

  NDRN is the nonprofit membership association for the Protection and Advocacy (P&A) systems and Client Assistance Programs (CAP) across the United States. P&As and CAPs provide legal advocacy and other services to individuals with disabilities, including assistance with special education issues. https://www.ndrn.org/

Conclusion

We hope this book has served as a comprehensive guide for child welfare workers who are seeking to become better advocates for children with disabilities in the child welfare system. Though this book may not make you an expert, as there is always more to learn about this complex system, we hope the content, vignettes, and resources have provided you a thorough overview of special education that is relevant to your work. We began by establishing the foundational understanding of special education, tracing its historical context, and explaining the key tenets, "gears," and procedures mandated by the Individuals with Disabilities Education Act (IDEA). We explored the fundamental principles of Free Appropriate Public Education (FAPE), the guarantee of a nondiscriminatory evaluation, and the importance of the Least Restrictive Environment (LRE). A central focus was placed on the Individualized Education Program (IEP), the cornerstone of special education, detailing its purpose, development, and essential components such as the Present Levels of Academic Achievement and Functional Performance (PLAAFP) and measurable annual goals. We also distinguished between IEPs and Section 504 Plans, highlighting their respective roles in ensuring appropriate educational opportunities.

Moving beyond the foundational knowledge, the book delved into the practical application of these principles. We emphasized the collaborative nature of the IEP process, identifying key participants and underscoring the importance of effective communication and conflict resolution. Recognizing the significant impact of trauma on the learning and development of children in the child welfare system, we dedicated a chapter to trauma-informed practices in education. Furthermore, we touched upon the unique considerations for students with high-intensity needs and those in early childhood special education settings. A critical aspect explored was transition planning, ensuring a smooth continuum of services as students progress through different educational stages and into postsecondary education, with an emphasis on person-centered planning and self-determination.

Finally, this chapter has equipped you with essential strategies to navigate common areas of disagreement among IEP teams and foster consensus-building using skills such as active listening, perspective-taking, and collaborative problem-solving to resolve conflicts related to the appropriateness and intensity of special education services. Understanding the formal dispute-resolution options available under IDEA, including mediation, resolution meetings, and due process hearings, provides additional avenues for advocacy when reaching a consensus proves challenging.

Throughout this book, the underlying message has been the vital role of the informed and empowered child welfare worker in ensuring that children under their care receive the free, appropriate public education they are legally entitled to. By understanding the legal framework, actively participating in the IEP process, considering the impact of trauma, planning effectively for transitions, and skillfully navigating disagreements, child welfare workers can serve as powerful advocates, bridging the gap between child welfare and special education systems. Your commitment to understanding and applying the principles and strategies outlined in these chapters will undoubtedly contribute to improved evidence-based decision-making, strengthened advocacy efforts, and, ultimately, better outcomes for the children and families you serve.

References

Burke, M. M., Magaña, S., Garcia, M., & Mello, M. P. (2016). Brief report: The feasibility and effectiveness of an advocacy program for Latino families of children with Autism Spectrum Disorder. *Journal of Autism and Developmental Disorders, 46*(7), 2532–2538. https://doi.org/10.1007/s10803-016-2765-x

CADRE. (2022). *IDEA dispute resolution parent guides.* Center for Appropriate Dispute Resolution in Special Education. https://www.cadreworks.org

Fish, W. W. (2008). The IEP meeting: Perceptions of parents of students who receive special education services. *Preventing School Failure: Alternative Education for Children and Youth, 53*(1), 8–14. https://doi.org/10.3200/PSFL.53.1.8-14

Fraser, M. W. (Ed.). (2004). *Risk and resilience in childhood: An ecological perspective* (2nd ed.). NASW Press.

Lake, J. F., & Billingsley, B. S. (2000). An analysis of factors that contribute to parent—school conflict in special education. *Remedial and Special Education, 21*(4), 240–251. https://doi.org/10.1177/074193250002100407

Trainor, A. A. (2010). Diverse approaches to parent advocacy during special education home—school interactions: Identification and use of cultural and social capital. *Remedial and Special Education, 31*(1), 34–47. https://doi.org/10.1177/0741932508324401

Yell, M. L., Katsiyannis, A., & Losinski, M. (2021). *Special education law* (4th ed.). Pearson.

Understood Team. (n.d.). *How to consent to some parts of an IEP and not others.* Understood. https://www.understood.org/en/articles/how-to-consent-to-some-parts-of-an-iep-and-not-others

Zirkel, P. A. (2020). An updated primer of special education law. *TEACHING Exceptional Children, 52*(4), 261–265. https://doi.org/10.1177/0040059919878671

About the Authors and Contributors

Authors

Kevin Monnin, PhD, is a project manager, nonprofit grant manager, and adjunct faculty. A former special education teacher in Virginia, Dr. Monnin's writing focuses on special education, policy, politics, and youth in foster care. He lives in Fairfax, VA, where he volunteers as a Court Appointed Special Advocate (CASA) supporting children, often with disabilities, who have experienced abuse and neglect.

Andrew M. Markelz, PhD, is an associate professor in the Department of Educational Foundations and Exceptionalities at James Madison University. He is founding editor of the Journal of Special Education Preparation and has authored five books pertaining to special education and advocacy. Dr. Markelz has served as a court appointed special advocate (CASA) for many years. Through research and practice, he is committed to expediting the novice-to-expert teaching curve by preparing special educators to implement proactive classroom management strategies and develop meaningful and legally defensible individualized education programs.

Contributors

Christy Berger graduated from Anderson University in 2006 with a bachelor's degree in social work. In 2008, she received her master's in social work from Indiana University Purdue University Indianapolis. Christy then obtained a post-master's certificate in school counseling in 2015. She was a social worker and school counselor for nine years before starting at the Indiana Department of Education as the Director of Social, Emotional and Behavioral Wellness. Christy now serves as the Executive Director of Student Services in Center Grove Schools, Indiana. She is passionate about creating positive whole-child focused school environments for each student.

Dr. Marla J. Lohmann is an associate professor and the program director for special education and alternative licensure programs at Colorado Christian University. She is actively involved in the fields of special education and early childhood education at both the state and national levels. Dr. Lohmann's research interests include innovations in teacher preparation, effective early childhood inclusion practices, and supporting the needs of students with disabilities in faith-based schools. Dr. Lohmann is the author of four books and more than three dozen articles on the topics of effective inclusion and teacher preparation.

Trapper Markelz writes from Arlington, Massachusetts. He is the author of the chapbook *Childproof Sky*, a Cherry Dress Chapbooks 2023 selection. His work has appeared in the journals *Baltimore Review*, *Dillydoun Review*, *Wild Roof Journal*, *Greensboro Review*, and *Passengers Journal*, among others.

Index